NASCAR

NASCAR CRAFTSMAN TRUCK SERIES

From Desert Dust to Superspeedways

JOHN CLOSE

MOTORBOOKS

DEDICATION

For my father, Lou Close, whose love of cars and dedication to racing placed my feet upon this path.

First published in 2007 by Motorbooks, an imprint of MBI Publishing Company, Galtier Plaza, Suite 200, 380 Jackson Street, St. Paul, MN 55101-3885 USA

Text copyright © 2007 by John Close
Photography copyright © 2007 by Nigel Kinrade, except where noted

To order more of our books, visit our website at www.motorbooks.com.

Front cover, left to right: Greg Biffle, Dennis Setzer, Jack Sprague, Mike Bliss, and Ted Musgrave. ***Main:*** Lined up for the start at Kansas Heartland Park in 2005.

Frontispiece: Tight action was the rule at Martinsville as Jason Small (No. 07) and Morgan Shepherd (No. 21) led this string of trucks into Turn One in the Advance Auto Parts 250 in 2002. *Nigel Kinrade*

Title pages: Packed together like a band of fighter jets, these trucks rumble through the tri-oval during the 2006 Daytona 250 at Daytona International Speedway. The NASCAR Craftsman Truck Series debuted at Daytona in 2000 and has been a Speedweeks fan favorite ever since. *High Sierra*

Acknowledgements page: Racing just inches apart at more than 180 miles per hour in the banking at Daytona International Speedway, Matt Crafton (No. 88), Rick Crawford (No. 14), Ron Hornaday Jr. (No. 33), and Kyle Busch (No. 15) show just how far the trucks have come since taking the green flag in 1994 at Mesa Marin Raceway in Bakersfield, California. *High Sierra*

Back cover, clockwise from top left: From the very beginning, the racing action in the new NASCAR Craftsman Truck Series was hot and heavy, as indicated by this three-wide shot of P. J. Jones (No. 1), Rick Carelli (No. 6), and Gary Ballough (No. 31) entering the first turn at Tucson. *High Sierra*

With the half-time break rule now just a distant memory, NASCAR Craftsman Truck Series teams were fielding top-notch pit crews by the 2002 season. Here, Jason Leffler's Ultra Motorsports crew springs into action during a pit stop at Martinsville. *Nigel Kinrade*

Mike Skinner hoists the winner's trophy over his head in the truck series' first Victory Lane ceremony at Phoenix. Skinner, who won eight times in the first year of the series, still counts this victory as one of the most important of his long racing career. *High Sierra*

ISBN-13: 978-0-7603-2659-6
ISBN-10: 0-7603-2659-2

Editors: Leah Noel and Nicole Edman
Designer: Brenda C. Canales

Printed in China

CONTENTS

Acknowledgments

The creation of this book could not have been possible without the efforts of many individuals who graciously gave time, information, guidance, and personal recollections to the project.

With that in mind, I would like to thank Owen Kearns, the only manager of communications in the history of the NASCAR Craftsman Truck Series, for his assistance in sorting out the mountain of details associated with this topic.

Additional thanks go out to Nigel Kinrade and Nate Mecha, whose photography was used to beautifully illustrate this volume.

Special thanks to Brian France, Dennis Huth, Wayne Auton, and all those who lent their recollections of the NASCAR Craftsman Truck Series to help the history of the division come alive within these pages.

Finally, many thanks to the staff at MBI Publishing Company, especially Leah Noel for her tireless efforts to make this book a reality, and to my wife, Gail, whose love and support over the years has allowed me to follow my racing dreams.

—John Close

Introduction

When the NASCAR Craftsman Truck Series powered its way onto the American motorsports landscape in 1994, the sanctioning body felt its newest venture had a lot of promise. At the time, NASCAR was winning the long-fought battle for motorsports supremacy in the United States and trumpeted the new series as a way to reach more stock car fans with big-league action at their local track. The division would be unique not only because it featured pickup trucks, not cars, but it also would bring a new brand of racing to short tracks in the heartland of the country, where the series would grow its own homegrown crop of heroes.

Yet, NASCAR knew the venture was a gamble. Would there be enough fan interest?

Was there a television audience for it? Would there be enough trucks and drivers to race? Could the series make money?

A dozen racing seasons later, the answer to all these questions has been a resounding yes. Not even the most optimistic of its initial supporters could have envisioned the success the NASCAR Craftsman Truck Series has enjoyed in today's world of American motorsports.

In the early years of the truck series, races were held at remote outposts like I-70, Evergreen, Tucson, Mesa Marin, Flemington, and Louisville Motor Speedway; however, nearly two-thirds of the races on the current series schedule are held in conjunction with NASCAR NEXTEL Cup events at legendary racetracks like

Tobey Butler (No. 12) fights to hold off Ken Schrader (No. 24) during the second NASCAR Craftsman Truck Series event at Tucson Raceway Park in 1994. Schrader was an early supporter of the division, later winning the third-ever regular season event at Saugus Speedway in 1995. *High Sierra*

Jason Leffler (No. 2) and Ted Musgrave (No. 1) formed a potent tandem for Jim Smith's Ultra Motorsports team in 2002. Musgrave, shown here battling Leffler at Darlington, won this event and two others that season. Meanwhile, Leffler, came up short of Victory Lane but did lead the division with eight pole positions. *High Sierra*

The NASCAR Craftsman Truck Series has always been "fan friendly"—especially in the early years when the division was looking to build a fan base. Here, driver Bob Keselowski signs a tire during one of the many autograph sessions held during the 1997 season. *High Sierra*

Daytona, Talladega, Atlanta, Texas, Las Vegas, Homestead-Miami, Dover, Michigan, and Lowe's Motor Speedway just north of Charlotte. The change from the short-track venues like 1–70, Evergreen, and Flemington to the larger tracks has helped boost event attendance figures from 400,000 in 1995—the first year of the series—to nearly 1.2 million in 2006.

Today, the NASCAR Craftsman Truck Series not only draws large, enthusiastic crowds to its events, but it is one of the most-watched racing series on television. For the February 2006 season opening race at Daytona, more than 1.1 million households tuned in to SPEED TV to see Mark Martin capture the checkered flag. Those viewership numbers made the telecast one of the highest-rated programs throughout all of the NASCAR Daytona Speedweeks events broadcast on SPEED. Today, the series ranks only behind its big brother NASCAR NEXTEL Cup Series and NASCAR Busch Series counterparts, outdistancing all other

Mike Skinner douses team owner Richard Childress with champagne in Victory Lane at Phoenix after winning the inaugural 1995 NASCAR Craftsman Truck Series championship. NASCAR NEXTEL Cup Series owners like Childress and Rick Hendrick were instrumental in getting the new division off the ground by fielding entries throughout the early years of the series. *High Sierra*

televised motorsports races in the coveted television rankings and brings in 70 million households of coverage in North America.

The concerns about finding drivers to participate in the series have also been overwhelmingly quelled. Current NASCAR NEXTEL Cup stars Greg Biffle, Carl Edwards, Kurt Busch, Scott Riggs, and Kevin Harvick all started their ascent to the sport's elite division in the truck series while former Cup dons Bobby Hamilton and Ted Musgrave have "retired" to truck racing and won championships there. The division has also delivered on growing its own stars as Ron Hornaday Jr., Mike Skinner, Jack Sprague, Terry Cook, Todd Bodine, and Rick Crawford are all synonymous with truck racing.

Drivers to win the NASCAR Craftsman Truck Series championship include Hornaday, Sprague, Skinner, and Hamilton, as well as Travis Kvapil and Mike Bliss.

In all, more than 500 different drivers had competed in a NASCAR Craftsman Truck Series event as the division entered the 2007 season.

Additionally, the truck series has created thousands of new opportunities in the big-league ranks of NASCAR for team crewmembers, shop personnel, administrative staffs, and public relations and marketing representatives. It has also opened up viable promotional opportunity for companies to showcase their products in a major motorsports series via live television.

In the end, the NASCAR Craftsman Truck Series would have never survived without great racing, which the division has certainly provided through a decade of door-to-door action, wild track battles, and down-to-the-wire photo finishes.

The events from the creation of the division to its popularity today are chronicled in the pages of this book, primarily told by the key individuals who lived them. It's an interesting story of how the simple idea of racing pickup trucks on oval tracks turned into a giant success story for NASCAR and those who work in, compete in, and follow racing as a sport.

Enjoy the ride.

Large pit areas and fancy garages weren't a part of the original NASCAR Craftsman Truck Series. The series' early days were characterized by cramped, short-track quarters, as evidenced by this team doing a gear change at a Tucson Winter Heat event in 1994. *High Sierra*

CHAPTER 1

An Idea Springs to Life in the Desert

The origins of the NASCAR Craftsman Truck Series weren't born on the confines of some local short-track oval, but rather in the wide-open desert spaces of the American Southwest. It was there—where trucks regularly competed in events like the Baja 1000—that the idea of creating a division where pickup trucks could compete on paved circle tracks came of age.

"There were four of us off-road truck racing for Ford Motor Company in the early 1990s and we wanted to showcase trucks better," said former longtime NASCAR Craftsman Truck Series team owner Jim Smith, who as a teenager worked for Junior Johnson's NASCAR team in the 1960s. "Having been around NASCAR a good part of my life, I knew there was no better way to showcase a truck than to put it on the racetrack at Daytona."

Smith, along with off-road racing buddies Frank "Scoop" Vessels, Jim Venable, and Dick Landfield, nurtured the idea of an oval track truck series and eventually built a truck to show executives at NASCAR. The truck debuted at the Circle Track Trade Show in Daytona Beach, Florida, in February 1994. While the vehicle drew plenty of attention from the show attendees, NASCAR's reaction to the new racing concept was one of caution.

"NASCAR hadn't developed anything new of a major magnitude for years," said Dennis Huth, who was NASCAR's vice president of administration in 1994. "At the time, a lot of the big tracks were being bought and sold and there

Brian France was just a fledgling in the "family business" when he dove headfirst into getting the new concept of a NASCAR truck series off of the ground. *Courtesy of NASCAR*

With his background as a guiding force in the NASCAR Winston Racing Series, Dennis Huth was a perfect choice to champion the new short-track efforts of the NASCAR Craftsman Truck Series in 1994. *High Sierra*

Longtime NASCAR NEXTEL Cup team owner Richard Childress was extremely interested in the truck on display at the original news conference to announce the division at Sears Point Raceway in 1994. Childress would eventually field a truck in the division and win the inaugural 1995 series championship with driver Mike Skinner. *High Sierra*

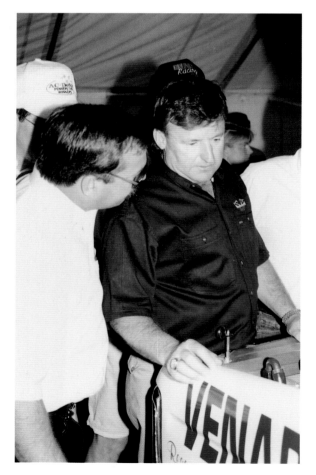

was a need for an entertainment package for all the short tracks. The trucks seemed like a viable opportunity. Brian [France] and I had quite a few conversations about it, but initially there wasn't much interest from upper management."

Despite the lukewarm reaction, France and Huth didn't let the idea die. They knew that vehicle sales data in the early 1990s showed the truck fleet was the largest growing transportation segment in the United States. Once the backbone of America's commercial transportation industry, trucks were now also a popular choice as a personal vehicle. France, who would eventually become NASCAR's board chairman and chief executive officer in 2003, could see the potential to capitalize on that with the new division.

"We were very excited about it," France said. "Trucks were being sold by all makes at a record number at that point. We were excited about launching a third national division. It seemed to fit."

Clearly, a lot of Americans were interested in pickup trucks and France kept the idea of a truck racing series alive in the halls of NASCAR's corporate headquarters.

"Brian and I eventually took the idea of a truck series back to Bill and Jim France and said we'd like to delve into this a little more and see what might become of it," Huth said.

Bill France Jr. agreed the concept had merit, and as a way to explore the idea further he directed Huth to set up a meeting in California with the four off-road truck racers who had come up with the proposal. Huth wasn't prepared for the reception that awaited him at the meeting, which was held at the Burbank Hilton.

"I was by myself and I thought there were going to be three or four people in the meeting," Huth said. "The original four guys were there, along with a bunch of other competitors. In all, I think there were about 15 of us in the meeting room."

The large gathering immediately indicated to Huth that there was significant interest in the project. He patiently listened as each of the series "founders" gave their take on the concept. Eventually, the conversation came around to money and how much NASCAR would be willing to pay for the concept. Huth told the assembled crowd that NASCAR had no interest in purchasing their dream, but that if they would allow NASCAR to take control of the idea, the sanctioning body would put all its organizational and marketing resources behind it.

The reaction to Huth's response was mixed, as all but Landfield were in favor of letting NASCAR steer the course of the new series. Landfield didn't want to give up the rights to the new product, but Smith convinced him and the group to go along with the NASCAR proposal.

"None of us had any expertise in running a racing series, but we were committed and well on our way to starting FastTruck USA [their own short-track truck racing series] before NASCAR said it wanted to take a look at it," Smith said. "Obviously, with the power behind NASCAR, [teaming with them] was the way to go. We weren't looking for any financial reward out of it; we were just looking to have a series."

With that, the group put Landfield in charge of ironing out the details of letting NASCAR take control of the idea with Huth, something they did the next morning. While NASCAR has built the series to what it is today, Smith, Landfield, Vessels, and Venable are remembered not only for coming up with the original idea of creating what would become the NASCAR Craftsman Truck Series, but for also helping establish the series throughout its early years.

"We'd have never made it without them," Huth said. "All of them supported the series

NASCAR NEXTEL Cup Series crew chief Steve Hmiel and NASCAR officials Gary Nelson and Dennis Huth share a laugh at the press conference announcing the formation of the NASCAR Craftsman Truck Series at Sears Point Raceway. *High Sierra*

Here's a front view of the first-ever NASCAR truck: a 1994 Ford F-150. Note the stock-appearing configuration of the front grill and bumper. The factory look was no accident as NASCAR and the truck's builders wanted to stir as much interest as possible from Detroit truck manufacturers. *High Sierra*

The first NASCAR truck featured a stock Ford F-150 pickup truck body that was ordered directly from the factory. California racer Gary Collins and North Carolina chassis builder Ron Hutcherson constructed the original series vehicle. *High Sierra*

Note the flat tailgate specially fabricated for the original NASCAR truck. It was one of the few pieces of the body that wasn't stock on the ground-breaking vehicle. Also of note was the large rear spoiler, which was significantly larger than the NASCAR NEXTEL Cup Series and NASCAR Busch Series cars' spoilers at the time. *High Sierra*

Low and mean—that was the look of the first NASCAR Craftsman truck as it made its official debut at a press conference held at Sears Point Raceway in Sonoma, California, on May 14, 1994. This truck was also the vehicle that was displayed at the Circle Track Trade Show in Daytona Beach, Florida, in an effort to generate interest in the new racing concept. *High Sierra*

An Idea Springs to Life in the Desert

The reinforced triangulated roll-cage design for the new NASCAR Craftsman Truck Series took its cues from the NASCAR NEXTEL Cup Series cars of the time. Here's a close-up look at an early example—the 1995 Spears Manufacturing No. 75 Chevy. *High Sierra*

from day one by fielding trucks in the early years and contributing untold personal time and money to establish the division. Their contribution can't be overlooked."

Spartan and spacious compared to today's modern, cramped NASCAR cockpits, the interior of the 1995 Spears Manufacturing Chevrolet was consistent with the times. Of note here are the NASCAR NEXTEL Cup Series–inspired gauge array, the minimal padding on the roll cage, and the door-bar construction on the right side of the vehicle. *High Sierra*

The concept of a NASCAR-supported truck series quickly gained momentum as track promoters began to express interest in the possibility of hosting events in an effort to expand their fan base. The interest at the track level was strongest on the West Coast, where various forms of truck racing were already established and where Huth had connections to several raceways thanks to his administrative role with the NASCAR Weekly Racing Series.

In rapid order, NASCAR pulled together division rules, race dates, venues, and sanctioning agreements.

"Brian [France] and I came up with using exhibition races to develop a business plan and a timeline for the series," Huth said. "We actually developed the plan on an airplane one day. We picked the tracks. All of them were West Coast tracks because that's where the majority of things were taking place. Mesa Marin, Saugus, Tucson, and Portland all had an interest in generating a new product, so this was kind of a let's-see- where-it-goes kind of thing. Our thoughts were that exhibitions would help us gain interest not only from the crowds, but from the competitors."

Finally it was time to announce the series to the rest of the world. That announcement came at Sears Point Raceway (now known as Infineon Raceway) on May 14, 1994. A hard rainstorm earlier in the day nearly washed away the event where Huth, Brian France, and Bill France Jr. eventually stepped to the podium to discuss the newest NASCAR vehicle and series. The trio detailed that the new division would debut in just a little more than two months in a series of exhibition races, the first to be held at Mesa Marin on July 30.

One of the first questions from the media on hand was how many trucks had been built and if they were ready to race.

"Bill [France Jr.] turned to me and asked how many we had," Huth said. "I pointed to

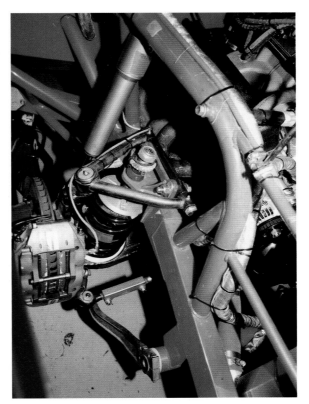

Take a peek at the front suspension of a modern NASCAR Craftsman Truck Series vehicle and it doesn't look much different than what is shown here on this 1995 inaugural season model. The front clip and chassis components of the new trucks were copied from those run then in the NASCAR NEXTEL Cup Series, utilizing the same upper and lower A-frames, springs, shocks, and brake packages. *High Sierra*

The original powerplant selected for the NASCAR Craftsman Truck Series was a 9:1 compression 358-cubic-inch V-8 engine that produced about 650 horsepower when outfitted with a four-barrel carburetor. The lower-compression engine was instituted as a nod to keeping costs under control by giving the series a powerplant that could be raced multiple times before a refresh or replacement was needed. *High Sierra*

The First Trucks

In addition to developing a race structure, finding tracks for events, recruiting drivers, and marketing the series, NASCAR had one more very large obstacle to overcome in making the NASCAR Craftsman Truck Series a reality—producing the trucks themselves.

According to Gary Collins, builder of the initial truck that was displayed at the Circle Track Trade Show in Daytona Beach, there was plenty of lively discussion as to just what a NASCAR truck should be.

"Jim Smith, Frank Vessels, Jim Venable, and Dick Landfield . . . initially wanted it to look like an off-road or stadium truck and have features like a mid-engine. I told them that kind of package wouldn't work on ovals and that NASCAR NEXTEL Cup Series was the number one form of automobile racing in the country at the time. They had a pretty basic pavement package, and I suggested we take that package, change the roll cage around a little, and put a pickup truck body on it," Collins said.

Collins also knew that Ford and Chevy were more likely to participate in the series if the race truck looked like one of their street offerings.

Once he persuaded the group to abandon its dreams of putting off-road-style vehicles on ovals, he began working on building the body of the first truck around the NASCAR NEXTEL Cup car chassis specifications.

"It was simple to do because everything was pretty much there," he said. "We got Ford to give us a truck body right off the assembly line without the inner panels on it. We got the fenders, doors, cab, and the rest of it from the factory—just skinned. We got it shipped to Charlotte, North Carolina . . . where Ron Hutcherson and I started welding the body together. We didn't cheat or flange it up. We just butted the doors and cab and everything else we had and welded it up."

Collins and Hutcherson mounted the completed body on a NASCAR NEXTEL Cup Series chassis and it fit just fine.

"The reason a truck chassis wheelbase is 112 inches long and a NASCAR NEXTEL Cup car is 110 is because that's what a Ford truck body fit. It fit like a glove," Collins said. "The entire interior was done like a NASCAR NEXTEL Cup car. Everything we did was built around the Cup car concept. It was really easy and it all came together simply."

Collins had the vehicle shipped back to his Mesa Marin shop to complete the construction. There, he and his crew created a fiberglass mold for the truck's front bumper and rear rolled tailgate pan to complete the body package.

The installed body on the prototype chassis had a modified roll cage extended for the truck's cab height that rose to 59 inches, significantly taller than the 51-inch NASCAR NEXTEL Cup roof height. Other striking visual differences between the two vehicles were the truck's squared-off look; long, flat-back bed-covered bed liner; and the significantly larger spoiler.

Under the hood, the truck was outfitted with a NASCAR NEXTEL Cup 358-cubic-inch engine with 9.5:1 compression ratio. The "more repeatable" (i.e., it could be used for multiple races) truck engine was installed to save the racers money and would still be plenty fast, putting out only 70 horsepower less than its 12:1 compression NASCAR NEXTEL Cup Series counterpart.

Both vehicles weighed 3,400 pounds without the driver. The rest of the truck racer's specifications were kissing cousins to a NASCAR NEXTEL Cup car, as the truck employed the same suspension, steering, braking and running gear parts, and electrical systems and gauges as those in the NASCAR NEXTEL Cup Series car template.

The construction techniques used in the car chassis were also mirrored in the truck's roll cage and safety bars, as well as the latest NASCAR driver safety initiatives. In short, save for a few incremental differences, the emerging NASCAR Craftsman truck was basically going to be a NASCAR NEXTEL Cup Series car with a truck body on it.

Now finished, the last piece of the puzzle was to test the prototype vehicle. Collins proved to be the perfect man for the job, as both driver and family track owner.

"I had sat on the pole for a Winston West race at Mesa Marin about three months before testing the truck and had run a 19.30-second lap in [that] car," Collins said. "Right out of the box, the truck ran a 19.60. I was surprised. It drove excellently. I had taken the same setup out of my [Winston] West car and applied it to the truck. By the end of the day, we were as fast in the truck as the car. It drove really well."

Collins' successful test run was the final detail needed to push forward with the project. NASCAR quickly approved the prototype truck.

Collins was immediately put to work building four additional trucks for the exhibition races. NASCAR, meanwhile, publicized the newly minted vehicle's rule specifications, making it possible for any chassis builder to start producing vehicles for the emerging NASCAR Craftsman Truck Series.

"As long as the truck conformed to the specifications we had determined, anyone could build one," former NASCAR Craftsman Truck Series director Dennis Huth said. "We were constantly working with the teams and the builders to make sure they were building what we wanted. We had to have a close working relationship to get them to continue to build the kind of trucks we needed from both a legal and safety standpoint."

The partnership worked. By mid-November, there were enough trucks to fill 16 starting spots in the first Winter Heat race. Just three months later, 33 trucks took the green flag in the February 5, 1995, inaugural NASCAR Craftsman Truck Series event at Phoenix.

The worries about having enough trucks to compete were over. In less than a year, the vehicle went from designing a concept and constructing a prototype, to testing and certifying it for competition, and to building race trucks and successfully competing with them.

The early concept for the NASCAR Craftsman Truck Series was to create a division where average Joe racers—guys like these attending to the two Fords owned by Jim Venable Racing prior to the Portland exhibition event—could participate in a big-league NASCAR touring series.
High Sierra

the prototype truck we had sitting on one of those auto show turntables and told him 'You're looking at it.' Bill then said, 'We got one—next question.'"

After the announcement, racing observers speculated on whether truck racing would be accepted throughout the industry, much less be a hit with the ticket-buying public.

"I remember H.A. "Humpy" Wheeler [president at Lowe's Motor Speedway in Charlotte] telling me that if he wanted to see trucks race, he'd go out and stand by the interstate," said Jerry Punch, a NASCAR NEXTEL Cup broadcaster in 1994 who later became the voice of the NASCAR Craftsman Truck Series when it aired on ESPN and ESPN2.

"At the time the trucks started, there was a lot of discussion about other promoters outside of NASCAR looking at ways to start up another stock car series. There was a glut of talented

Craftsman was active in the series from the very beginning, serving as a presenting sponsor of the 1995 season before becoming the entitlement sponsor the following year. Here, the company struts its stuff with a huge sign inside Turn Four at the first Phoenix race in 1995.
High Sierra

drivers running around the short tracks who had some name exposure," Punch added. "By starting the truck series, NASCAR was able to gobble up those drivers and team owners."

Despite the doubts, the new venture pushed forward with driver/truck builder Gary Collins working nearly around the clock at his shops located outside Mesa Marin Raceway in Bakersfield, California, to construct four additional trucks that would compete in the first exhibition race. Meanwhile, NASCAR was encouraging drivers, teams, and racetracks to sign on for a 20-race series that would debut at Phoenix International Raceway on February 5, 1995.

"It's always so tough when you start something from scratch, and our biggest concern early on was making sure we would have enough equipment at the races," Huth said. "It wasn't like a stock car series where if you had a short field of cars, you could get some like-kind cars from a technical aspect and fill out the field. We

couldn't do that with the trucks because they were so unique. We were dealing with something totally different, so we had to be very careful as to how we sold the idea of racing trucks and how we worked the process. Fortunately, since it was a NASCAR project, chassis and truck builders were confident they could move forward with the construction of the trucks."

All that was left was to put the product on the racetrack.

"The biggest problem you have in launching anything—back then or today—is how competitive the existing sports landscape already is," France said. "We were launching the NASCAR Craftsman Truck Series just about the time the WNBA was coming on line. Major league soccer was making its North American push and IRL and CART were contemplating bumping around. To break through with something new on a national basis was a very tall order."

From the very beginning, the racing action in the new NASCAR Craftsman Truck Series was hot and heavy, as indicated by this three-wide shot of P. J. Jones (No. 1), Rick Carelli (No. 6), and Gary Ballough (No. 31) entering the first turn at Tucson. *High Sierra*

CHAPTER 2

Taking the Green Flag

With the musical theme from *2001: A Space Odyssey* blaring over the track speakers and fireworks filling the air, the NASCAR Craftsman Truck Series debuted at Mesa Marin on Saturday, July 30, 1994. Billed as the Mesa Marin 20, the inaugural exhibition event featured five trucks in a 20-lap shootout on the half-mile paved oval.

"Tonight you are witnessing a very historic occasion and the birth of the next great NASCAR racing series," Dennis Huth told the large crowd on hand for the event. "This is just a glimpse of what will be a national touring series in 1995."

Gary Collins, driving one of the trucks he built, set fast time for the race, turning in a lap of 19.731 seconds. P. J. Jones (son of famed Indy car driver Parnelli Jones), Craig Huartson, Dave Ashley, and Rob MacCachren joined Collins in the starting field.

Officially, there were four lead changes in the inaugural exhibition race, the last when Jones assumed the point on Lap 14. From there, it was smooth sailing as he cruised to the win in the all green-flag race that took just seven minutes to complete. Jones averaged

81.818 miles per hour and earned first-place prize money totaling $900. Collins hung on for second with MacCachren, Huartson, and Ashley completing the final finishing order. Each was awarded $800 for his efforts.

"Everyone from Daytona was there to see it," Collins said. "P. J. and I were the only ones with pavement experience and NASCAR didn't want us to make it look bad. They had everything choreographed out and they told us to get after it in the final 10 laps."

Curious fans look over the five trucks in the garage area prior to the running of the first NASCAR Craftsman Truck Series race at Mesa Marin Raceway in Bakersfield, California. While the initial exhibition event only lasted a little over seven minutes, it solidified the idea that trucks could put on a good racing program that would be accepted by the fans. *High Sierra*

Five drivers and trucks made history when they took to the track for the Mesa Marin 20 NASCAR Craftsman Truck Series race. Included in the group were original truck builder and NASCAR Winston West Series racer Gary Collins in the No. 12 Venable Racing Ford, Indy and sports car ace P. J. Jones behind the wheel of the No. 1 Vessels Stallion Farm Ford, desert and stadium truck racer Dave Ashley in the No. 2 Dick Landfield Enduro Racing Ford, and off-road and stadium racer Rob MacCachren in the No. 21 Venable Racing Ford. The lone Chevrolet in the field was entered by Bunce Huartson Racing and driven by Craig Huartson. All but Collins led the 20-lap race. Jones passed MacCachren on the 14th lap while en route to the historic victory. *High Sierra*

One of the early attractions of the NASCAR Craftsman Series was the simplicity of the venture. Note the few numbers and dress of Dave Ashley's crewmembers as they attend to the No. 2 Ford prior to the second exhibition race at Portland on August 20, 1994. *High Sierra*

"These trucks were unproven and we didn't want anyone going out there and busting their butts," Dennis Huth said, explaining NASCAR's competition request for the event. "We didn't want any wrecks or breakdowns because we only had five trucks."

In the end, Collins and Jones drove their hardest over the final laps in an effort to have their names written into the history books as the first winner in the new division.

"They said that they wanted us to put on a good show," Jones said. "They wanted to see some good side-by-side racing early, and then in

the last 10 laps, it was a free for all. . . . Personally, I thought that would be a pretty good race to win considering it was the first-ever race. It was the kind of thing people would remember."

"People still come up to me today and want to talk about the truck series because they know I won the first race," he added. "It's part of NASCAR history."

"I ran two inches off of P. J.'s bumper and side-by-side with him for the final 10 laps," said Collins, who ironically was the only one of the five drivers in the race not to lead the event. "I remember the place was packed and people

Dave Ashley's No. 2 Ford was locked and loaded as its crew posed for this photo on the starting grid prior to the exhibition race at Portland Speedway. While Ashley was a fixture in the exhibition races, he made just one career start in an official NASCAR Craftsman Truck Series race. He finished 30th—last—in the 1995 Ford Credit 125 at Mesa Marin after his Ultra Wheels Ford suffered engine failure on Lap 77. *High Sierra*

loved it. They went crazy. Everyone could relate to these trucks. At that time, there wasn't a truck series alive anywhere and people were amazed at how fast the trucks were and how well they drove."

The second race at Portland (Oregon) Speedway saw MacCachren, former winner of the SCORE Baja 1000 and 500 off-road races, take the checkered flag. Collins finally drove his way into Victory Lane in the third exhibition event at Saugus Speedway in Santa Clarita, California. Then two-time NASCAR Featherlite Southwest Tour late-model stock car champion Ron Hornaday Jr., driving the Spears Motorsports

Gary Collins rolled his Ford under the checkered flag to win the third NASCAR Craftsman Truck Series exhibition race at Saugus Speedway in California on September 10, 1994. Note the packed grandstand, even if it is only about 10 rows high. Collins, who was instrumental in steering the direction of the new series vehicle design by taking cues from a NASCAR NEXTEL Cup Series car, is also shown here being interviewed by announcer Larry Naston after the event. *High Sierra*

With the assistance of television outlets like TNN (The Nashville Network), the NASCAR Craftsman Truck Series was beamed into homes everywhere, bringing the division instant recognition with the racing public. *High Sierra*

Chevrolet, claimed the final exhibition event at Tucson (Arizona) Raceway Park.

The artistic and competitive success of the exhibition events had Huth and Brian France on full throttle to plan three more races at Tucson over the winter of 1994 and 1995. Unlike the exhibitions, these races would feature expanded fields and race lengths. These would be full-fledged races, and thanks to TNN (The Nashville Network) they would no longer be a regional West Coast novelty.

"We had credibility with TNN and others to give us an opportunity to showcase the new series," France said. "If it were anybody else in motorsports, it might not have gotten that credibility. Having television on our side was very helpful."

The 200-lap Winter Heat races featured a half-time break at the 100-lap mark—a 10-minute stoppage of the action to take the place of live pit stops so crews could make adjustments to the vehicles.

"It was an exciting time in NASCAR," said Wayne Auton, the current NASCAR Craftsman

Craig Huartson, driving the No. 8 truck, and Ken Schrader, behind the wheel of the No. 24 truck, lead a pack of trucks into the first turn at Tucson Raceway Park during the Winter Heat series in 1994. On average, the Winter Heat races drew 15 to 20 trucks per event and showed racers were willing to invest in the new division by building and racing the series. *High Sierra*

These drivers photos were taken at the second NASCAR Craftsman Truck Series race of the 1995 season at Tucson. They are among the first driver headshots taken for the series. Drivers pictured are (this page, top row) P. J. Jones, Wayne Jacks, and Mike Bliss; (this page, bottom row) John Kinder and Mike Hurlbert; (opposite page, top row) Bob Keselowski, Johnny Benson Jr., and Jack Sprague; (opposite page, bottom row) Jerry Glanville, Ron Hornaday Jr., and Tobey Butler. *High Sierra*

P. J. Jones was all smiles as he poses with the Tucson Raceway trophy queen after winning the second Winter Heat event on December 11, 1994. Jones took home $7,325 of the $37,200 total purse posted for the event. *High Sierra*

Owen Kearns was a California sportswriter and road-racing enthusiast when he took a job in the NASCAR West Coast offices in 1983. Kearns would eventually become the manager of communications for the NASCAR Craftsman Truck Series and has been the only person to serve in that capacity since the inception of the series. *John Close*

Truck Series director. "There had been a truck series kind of deal that was run on the outskirts of NASCAR back in the 1980s—even Mike Helton owned one of them. The trucks that were designed at that time were totally different than anything that we started running in 1994 and 1995. This was new and exciting."

An indication as to just how far the series had come from the exhibitions was that 16 trucks took the green flag for the first Tucson Winter Heat event on Sunday, November 20, 1994. Also expanded were the small purses of the exhibition races: the inaugural SuperTruck 200 posted awards of $37,200.

Mike Skinner pits the No. 3 GM Goodwrench Chevy during the inaugural 1995 NASCAR Craftsman Truck Series race at Phoenix International Raceway. Note the capacity crowd that filled the raceway that day to see the trucks compete as part of the annual Copper World Classic event. *High Sierra*

Mike Skinner, in his first ride for Richard Childress Racing, sat on the pole and led the first 62 laps before giving way to Rick Carelli. The two drivers swapped the lead with Ron Hornaday Jr. a total of seven times before Carelli took the lead for good with 25 laps remaining, rolling to the win in the Total Petroleum–sponsored Chevy. P. J. Jones managed to work his way into the runner-up spot in the final laps with Hornaday, Dirk Stephens, and Johnny Benson Jr. completing the top five.

Only three trucks didn't finish the 75-lap event, one of them driven by Robby Gordon.

The solid on-track performance and an inquisitive television audience bolstered the hopes of the NASCAR brass that the series would be a success.

"If you had to say what was the defining moment that helped the [NASCAR Craftsman] Truck Series turn the corner I would say it was the Winter Heat races," Jones said. "They held them in the middle of winter when nothing else was happening. The fact that there was no other racing on television to watch was big, and they turned out to be very popular shows with the fans. That exposure gave the truck series the kick start and the attention it needed heading into the first season."

Mike Skinner hoists the winner's trophy over his head in the NASCAR Craftsman Truck Series' first Victory Lane ceremony at Phoenix. Skinner, who won eight times in the first year of the series, still counts this victory as one of the most important of his long racing career. *High Sierra*

While the Winter Heat races had proven the new truck series could put on good short-distance races on bullrings like Tucson Raceway Park, racing at the one-mile Phoenix International Raceway—the site of the division's first-ever regular season event—was something completely different.

"We didn't really know what was going to happen at that first race in Phoenix," said Owen Kearns, NASCAR Craftsman Truck Series manager of communications. "We had held the exhibition races and we had 15 trucks or so at each race. We had a few that were pretty good and we had some that weren't too good. We didn't know if we were going to have a full field for the first series race at Phoenix or not."

With the TNN television cameras rolling and a big crowd on hand, the GM Goodwrench 200—the debut of the NASCAR Craftsman Truck Series—got under way. The February 5, 1995, event was held in conjunction with the Copper World Classic, a multidivision racing spectacular that had been held each year at Phoenix since 1977.

NASCAR's fears of not having enough vehicles on hand proved to be unfounded as 33 trucks—17 Chevys, 13 Fords, and 3 Dodges—took the green flag under perfect sunny and warm conditions.

Hornaday, driving the Dale Earnhardt–owned No. 16 RCCA Products Chevy, led the field to the starter's flag and paced the first 32 laps after winning the pole position with a speed of 123.665 miles per hour. Meanwhile, El Cajon, California, driver John Borneman earned the distinction of being the first to drop out of a NASCAR Craftsman Truck Series event when his Chevrolet experienced steering problems on Lap 22.

Back up front, Hornaday was battling NASCAR NEXTEL Cup Series stars Terry Labonte, Ken Schrader, Geoffrey Bodine, and Johnny Benson Jr. for the top spot. Back in the

Ron Hornaday Jr. (No. 16) and Rick Carelli (No. 6) battle for position during the final laps at the second race of the 1995 season at Tucson Raceway Park. Hornaday—the all-time wins leader in the NASCAR Craftsman Truck Series—went on to score his first division triumph at Tucson and later celebrated with crew chief Doug Richert and the Tucson Raceway trophy queen. *High Sierra*

The drivers' accessibility to the fans was a big part of selling the NASCAR Craftsman Truck Series to the public. Here, Dave Rezendes signs an autograph for a fan prior to the race at Saugus Speedway in 1995. *High Sierra*

Pit road was a crowded, busy place during the half-time break at the 1995 Jerr Dan/Nelson 150 at Evergreen Speedway. In the foreground are the trucks of Walker Evans (No. 20), Dave Rezendes (No. 7), and former NFL coach Jerry Glanville (No. 81). *High Sierra*

To say the garage area was a relaxed place in the early days of the NASCAR Craftsman Truck Series is an understatement. Here, a woman takes a nap among the pit equipment at Evergreen Speedway in 1995. *High Sierra*

Can you say four wide? The back straight turn at Louisville Motor Speedway made for tight quarters for this group, which included Randy Churchill (No. 88), Mike Skinner (No. 3), and Joe Ruttman (No. 84) in 1995. *High Sierra*

It was every man for himself in an escape to miss this wild melee on the front stretch of the Milwaukee Mile in 1995. *High Sierra*

After years of working in other NASCAR divisions, Wayne Auton joined the NASCAR Craftsman Truck Series at Milwaukee in 1995. Auton, shown here at that Milwaukee event, continues as the series director. *High Sierra*

pack, Mike Skinner was fighting to catch up with the leaders.

"When we got to Phoenix for the first points race, we were really fast. Then we dropped a valve in the engine in qualifying and we started the race way in the back," Skinner said. "Richard [Childress] told me I would have to be patient and that I probably wouldn't beat the NASCAR NEXTEL Cup guys in the field."

But Skinner's black No. 3 Richard Childress Racing entry—painted to mirror Dale Earnhardt's famed NASCAR NEXTEL Cup car—proved to be more than a field filler as he drove through the pack to take the lead for good on Lap 62 of the 80-lap race.

At the finish, Skinner put his name in the history books as the first winner of a truck series regular-season event by nipping Labonte by a

Butch Miller gets a big hug and kiss from his wife, Donna, after winning the NASCAR Craftsman Truck Series race at Colorado National Speedway in 1995. Miller beat Mike Skinner to the line by 0.001 of a second to earn his only career truck series victory. *High Sierra*

scant 0.09 of a second. Schrader held on for third with Joe Bessey and Geoffrey Bodine completing the top-5 finishers.

"I was real careful getting up through the field, and the next thing you know, we have a truck that's capable of winning the race," Skinner said. "It came down to the last lap and I almost wrecked coming off of Turn Four, but somehow

This crewmember gets down and dirty as he works on the No. 25 Chevy driven by Jack Sprague at Martinsville in 1995. Teams still do their race prep on pit road at Martinsville, one of the shortest tracks on the circuit, measuring just 0.526-miles in length. *High Sierra*

I held on to it and we won the first race. It was a time in my life where I had struggled to get my name out there for 20 years, and then overnight I became a household name. . . . It was pretty weird, but it was pretty cool, too."

As the season progressed, the series continued to find a solid audience at the track. More important, fans across the country were getting interested in the new series, tuning in as TNN and CBS brought the division into living rooms everywhere. To the viewer at home, the solid on-track battles highlighted by photo finishes like the

one between Skinner and Labonte in the season-opening race at Phoenix or the 0.0001-second win Butch Miller posted over Skinner at Colorado National Speedway in July were as good or better than anything the fans were watching in the NASCAR NEXTEL Cup Series races on Saturday nights or Sunday afternoons.

Heading into the 20th and final race of the year—the GM Goodwrench/Delco Battery 200 at Phoenix—Skinner had built an 88-point lead in the championship standings on the strength of seven wins, something that didn't go

Geoffrey Bodine was a frequent visitor to the NASCAR Craftsman Truck Series, competing in 10 of the 20 events on the 1995 schedule. Bodine, shown here before the North Wilkesboro event, finished in the top five six times, including placing third at the North Carolina speedway. *High Sierra*

Rick Johnson spins the No. 01 truck in Turns Three and Four, setting off a big accident at Mesa Marin in the second-to-last series event of the 1995 season. Johnson, seven-time AMA Motorcross Champion, recovered to finish 25th in the event. *High Sierra*

unnoticed with owner Richard Childress. The winner of multiple NASCAR NEXTEL Cup titles with driver Dale Earnhardt wanted another championship trophy to add to the team's collection back in Welcome, North Carolina.

Childress attended four of the last four of five races, offering the truck team his input on how to capture the title. But his advice didn't always seem to make sense to Skinner.

"At Sears Point, the third to last race, I had the truck that could win the race," Skinner said. "The team hounded me on the radio all day telling me to slow down, slow down, slow down. Ronnie [Hornaday] came up and they told me to pull over and let him go because he might wreck us and we would lose the championship."

After the race, Skinner's team was excited about his third-place finish, while Skinner was mad—knowing he could have won that race.

"Richard told me they were going to teach me how to win a championship. We argued some about it, but after I won the next race at Mesa Marin, we only had to finish 23rd or better at Phoenix to win the championship."

Skinner wasn't the least bit interested in riding around to a sub-par finish in the final event at Phoenix. He led all but 34 of the 124 laps, including the final 59 to win the race and the championship. Ernie Irvan, another NASCAR NEXTEL Cup competitor who made four NASCAR Craftsman Truck Series starts during the inaugural season, finished second with Bodine, Ted Musgrave, and Hornaday completing the top-5 finishers in the season's final event.

In all, a total of 103 different drivers took the green flag during the division's inaugural season.

"I thought the inaugural year turned out excellent," Brian France said. "We secured Craftsman as

Mike Skinner was the trophy king in Victory Lane at Phoenix after winning the inaugural 1995 NASCAR Craftsman Truck Series championship. *High Sierra*

the entitlement sponsor and the television ratings were pretty good. The racing turned out to be and still remains some of the best we could have hoped for. A lot of people think, all things aside, that the truck series is the best racing that

NASCAR has. We were pretty excited about the first year and the progress we were making."

"You could look at it from all sides and see that the amount of effort everyone put forth to make the series a success was incredible,"

Richard Childress is flanked by his championship-winning drivers—seven-time NASCAR NEXTEL Cup title winner Dale Earnhardt and 1995 NASCAR Craftsman Truck Series kingpin Mike Skinner—at the season-ending series banquet. *High Sierra*

Dennis Huth said. "Drivers, teams, tracks, promoters, cities, and their officials—everyone contributed to the early success of the series, and I really believe that, in large part, is what made the series what it is today."

Jim Smith, one of the off-road racers who had dreamed up this new form of truck competition, was also impressed. "That first year was just like old-time stock car racing I remembered back in the 1960s," he said. "If somebody wrecked, you helped him. . . . There was really a lot of camaraderie. I think the [NASCAR Craftsman] Truck Series still has that more than any other NASCAR series. We were racing in little places like Monroe, Washington, and it was fun. We had a great time."

The field thunders down the front stretch in front of a huge crowd at Phoenix late in the 1996 season. By the end of its second year, the series had established itself as a viable motorsports property and was drawing big crowds wherever it went. *High Sierra*

CHAPTER 3

Beatin' and Bangin'

The earthy, early feel of the NASCAR Craftsman Truck Series that Jim Smith and the rest of the competitors felt during the early years of the division was due in large part to the places where the races were held.

Unlike the NASCAR NEXTEL Cup Series and NASCAR Busch Series counterparts that competed at race palaces like Texas, Bristol, and Charlotte, the truck events were held in remote outposts of the sport—places like Evergreen, Washington; Odessa, Missouri; Monroe, Washington; and Flemington, New Jersey.

More important than location or geography, however, was the configuration of these racetracks. With the exception of Phoenix, Milwaukee, and Sears Point, all of the truck races in 1995 were contested on tracks 0.745 of a mile in length or less. Some, like Colorado National and Tucson, measured as little as 0.375 of a mile long—slightly bigger than the average high school running track.

The cramped confines of these grassroots raceways not only harkened back to the 1960s when NASCAR's top division competed at bullrings in locales like Wilson and Hickory, North Carolina, and Greenville and Columbia, South Carolina, but they also produced the same kind of slam-bang racing NASCAR was known for decades earlier.

"Those early races had a Saturday-night feel on the short tracks—a lot of beatin' and bangin'," driver Jack Sprague said. "We'd knock the hell out of each other. The trucks didn't have and didn't need any aerodynamics. Didn't matter about the fenders, you didn't need 'em."

While the drivers exhibited a take-no-prisoners mentality on the track, they did everything they could to jointly promote the division off it. Many

From the very beginning, the NASCAR Craftsman Truck Series was known for its rock 'em sock 'em action. Here, Mike Bliss (No. 08), John Kinder (No. 14), Jerry Glanville (No. 81), and Sammy Swindell (No. 88) mix it up at I-70 Speedway near Odessa, Missouri, in 1995. *High Sierra*

The NASCAR Craftsman Truck Series made its first road course appearance on July 29, 1995, at Kansas Heartland Park in Topeka. Not only did the race prove the trucks could turn both left and right, but it also drew some interesting entries, including top NASCAR NEXTEL Cup Series team owner Rick Hendrick in the No. 25 Budweiser Chevy. Hendrick finished 23rd, falling out of the 60-lap event on the 49th circuit with transmission trouble. *High Sierra*

of the small towns hosting the NASCAR Craftsman Truck Series during those early seasons staged race festivals in conjunction with the events. The local newspapers were full of stories about the series coming to town while area radio stations competed to get on-air driver interviews.

Truck racing might not have made a media ripple in a big city like Atlanta or Philadelphia, but it was the only game in town in places like Flemington, New Jersey—estimated population, 3,800—and it was all residents there were talking about.

"I still think about racing at places like Flemington, Portland, and Monroe," driver Mike Bliss said. "Those were places that sat only 7,000 to 10,000 people, but no matter how many were there, they were really excited to see you. Everyone was crowded into these little tracks and you could really feel the energy of the people. Racing into the first corner at

Louisville Speedway and seeing the people in the swimming pool, or trying to not run over the manhole cover in Turn One at Portland, was pretty neat."

The barn-raising mentality of NASCAR and everyone associated with the new division had slowly built the truck series into a success— one that Craftsman Hand Tools was now fully behind. George Kurkowski, specialty marketing manager for Craftsman at the time, said the company made a commitment to the new NASCAR series because "NASCAR had proven that America's love affair with the automobile had shifted gears to include trucks."

Along with a title sponsor, the 1996 season marked the re-entry of Chrysler Corporation to the NASCAR ranks. A major factory supporter of NASCAR during the 1960s and 1970s, Chrysler folded its racing tent in the mid-80s. The path taken by Dodge from first providing vehicles for the NASCAR Craftsman Truck Series in 1996 and then adding its cars into the NASCAR NEXTEL Cup Series ranks in 2001 later served as a template for Toyota to do the same with its trucks in 2004 and cars in 2007.

Media exposure also expanded in 1996, thanks to Superstation WTBS joining the group of networks that broadcast NASCAR Craftsman Truck Series events. The television package also included CBS Sports, ESPN2, and TNN— virtually assuring that anyone with a television now had access to a truck race on the various

NASCAR NEXTEL Cup Series owner Felix Sabates fielded a truck for Wisconsin short-tracker Jay Sauter in seven 1996 NASCAR Craftsman Truck Series events. Sauter is shown here having overheating problems during the half-time break at Phoenix. Sauter, who qualified third, recovered to finish 11th in the 200-mile event. *High Sierra*

network or cable packages. Meanwhile, the Truck Broadcasting Network, a division of Motor Racing Network (MRN), was also beaming coverage of each race to its more than 400 MRN-affiliated radio stations. The NASCAR Craftsman Truck Series was packing both the grandstands and the airwaves, which also included a new, emerging user-friendly form of information and communication: the internet.

Those winds of change had NASCAR blowing the 1996 truck schedule in a different direction—south—to open the season at the Metro Dade Homestead Motorsports Complex (now Homestead-Miami Speedway).

Held on St. Patrick's Day, 1996, the Homestead race was the first in an expanded schedule that now counted 24 events. The race also hailed a change in philosophy, as NASCAR saw greater marketing potential by expanding the series into larger racetracks and media/marketing municipalities. The sanctioning body had tested the market for this new division in Tucson, Bakersfield, and Evergreen, where it played to packed houses. Supported by better-than-expected

Tobey Butler (No. 52) won the pole and led the field to the green flag in front of a packed house at Evergreen Speedway in 1996. It was outside front row driver Mike Bliss (No. 2) who won the event, however, leading 156 of the 200 laps contested that day. *High Sierra*

television numbers, NASCAR had all the proof it needed to start moving the series on to bigger and better venues.

Competitively, that meant the 1.53-mile Homestead track would be the largest oval the trucks had run on to date. Along with the one-mile ovals at Milwaukee, New Hampshire, and Phoenix, the 1-mile Nazareth (Pennsylvania) Speedway was added to the scheduling mix. Two additional road course events were included in the schedule—one at Watkins Glen (New York) Raceway and the other at Heartland

Park Topeka (Kansas)—turning the trucks to the right three times that season, the third coming at Sears Point.

The real cherry on the schedule, as if starting the season under tropical Florida skies wasn't enough, came at the end of the season when the trucks would be the first of NASCAR's top three divisions to compete on the newly completed 1.5-mile Las Vegas Motor Speedway.

Suddenly, the trucks were showcased on some serious tracks—now 7 of 24 events would be held on oval tracks of a mile or more in

Bryan Reffner came out of the American Speed Association (ASA) ranks to win the 1996 NASCAR Craftsman Truck Series Raybestos Rookie of the Year award. Driving for Mark Simo and Ernie Irvan, Reffner proved he would be a contender early by winning the pole position for the fifth race of the year at Tucson. Reffner finished 11th in the event, despite spinning out. *Nigel Kinrade/High Sierra*

length. The transformation to a superspeedway division had begun—a revision that would climax four years later with the first truck series race at Daytona in 2000.

The diversity of the tracks didn't seem to matter to Ron Hornaday Jr. as he wheeled the Dale Earnhardt Inc. NAPA Auto Parts Chevy to the 1996 season championship. Hornaday proved his versatility mastering the short tracks with wins at Portland and Louisville, but he also won on the road course at Watkins Glen and captured a speedway race at New Hampshire.

Thanks to a 72-point lead over Mike Skinner, Hornaday entered the final race at Las Vegas needing to finish just 18th or better to win the title. In a division that just a little over a year ago was concerned about having enough

Doug George (No. 21), Walker Evans (No. 20), and Kenny Allen (No. 65) tangle on the back straight curve in the 1996 NASCAR Craftsman Truck Series race at Louisville Motor Speedway. Ron Hornaday Jr. won for the second time that season, with Mike Skinner, Jimmy Hensley, Dave Rezendes, and Joe Ruttman completing the top-5 finishers. *High Sierra*

It was a Ford versus Chevrolet battle as a large crowd looked on at the start of the 1996 Sears Auto Center 200 at Wisconsin State Fair Park in Milwaukee. Polesitter Mike Bliss in the No. 2 Ford and Mike Skinner's No. 3 Chevrolet were no match for Jack Sprague's mount as Sprague captured his second victory in a row and the third in 10 NASCAR Craftsman Truck Series events that season. *High Sierra*

Beatin' and Bangin'   53

In a strange twist to the 1996 truck series race at Watkins Glen International, Steve Park won the pole for the event but never took the green flag. Park, shown here at the Busch Pole Award board, subbed for Joe Nemechek during qualifying and rolled to the top spot with an average speed of 115.379 miles per hour. Nemechek showed up the next day, started at the back of the 31-truck field, and finished second behind Ron Hornaday Jr. *High Sierra*

vehicles to race, a record 61 trucks showed up to try to make the 40-truck field for the Vegas event. Eventual Raybestos Rookie of the Year award winner Bryan Reffner won the pole with the fastest lap in the history of the division up to that point—157.909 miles per hour. Sprague stomped his way to a win for Hendrick Motorsports by beating Bill Elliott, Joe Ruttman, Michael Waltrip, and Dave Rezendes to the checkered flag.

Hornaday finished 10th and captured the title by a 3,831 to 3,778 margin over Sprague, who had to be satisfied with a Vegas winner's check of $79,825 and jumping past Skinner in the final standings to the runner-up position.

For Hornaday, winning the title was an overwhelming experience.

"We were at the last race in Vegas and Dale [Earnhardt] was spotting for me," he said. "I remember him telling me 'We got you this far,

Kenny Irwin won the first and only NASCAR Craftsman Truck Series pole position of his career at Richmond in 1996. Irwin, behind the wheel of the No. 62 Raybestos Ford, is shown here battling eventual race winner Mike Skinner for position during the race in which Irwin finished fifth.
High Sierra

The rains came to North Wilkesboro in 1996, delaying the start of the Lowe's 250 NASCAR Craftsman Truck Series race. In the end, it turned out to be a bright day for Jack Roush and Mark Martin as the pair won their first career series event.
High Sierra

now the rest is up to you.' Talk about having all the pressure on your shoulders. But they gave me the best stuff—best truck, best engines, best financing. It was overwhelming to win the championship and have Dale down there pushing everyone aside when I was climbing out of the truck to give me a hug and tell me 'You da man, you da man!' "

Two additional stats stick out for Hornaday about that 1996 season. The Palmdale, California, driver finished in the top 10 in 23 of the 24 events and won $625,634 in prize money. Not bad considering a little over two years earlier, the entire payout for the first exhibition truck race at Bakersfield was $4,100.

While Hornaday was taking the major bows at the end of 1996, others such as Skinner,

Sprague, Bliss, Rich Bickle, Butch Miller, and Rick Carelli were making names for themselves in the racing world as NASCAR Craftsman Truck Series drivers. They had become the series' promised homegrown crop of new, rugged NASCAR stars.

"Back then, the NASCAR Busch Series guys were really complaining about the NASCAR NEXTEL Cup guys coming in and stealing their thunder," Skinner said. "All of us in the NASCAR Craftsman Truck Series were saying 'C'mon, bring it on.' We enjoyed having guys like Mark Martin, Ernie Irvan, and Kenny Schrader coming over and racing with us because they were in our backyard then and we could beat them sometimes. We beat them a lot. I'd beat them, Hornaday would beat them, Sprague would beat them. It was a really neat atmosphere for a bunch of guys trying to make a name for themselves."

In 1997, more change was on tap for the burgeoning NASCAR Craftsman Truck Series—more big tracks would be added to the schedule while birthplace venues would fall off the tour.

Skinner, the division's first superstar, would also leave, graduating to the NASCAR NEXTEL Cup Series ranks—the first truck driver to do so. His record of 16 wins, 15 poles, 7 outside poles, one championship, and over $1 million in earnings in 44 races over two seasons fueled his rise. Over the next seven years, Skinner would make 214 career NASCAR NEXTEL Cup starts, earning nearly $13 million in the process. He eventually came back to the truck racing in 2004 as one of the leaders of the Toyota vanguard.

Looking back at those frenetic first two seasons, Skinner fondly recalls the short-track races that launched the NASCAR Craftsman Truck Series.

"You can't take anything away from Texas, Charlotte, and Atlanta. Those places are first-class facilities and it's neat to run trucks around them at 190 miles per hour. But then going to Monroe [Washington] Speedway was awesome. Portland didn't even have a wall around it. If you went off the track in Turn Three, you were out in the thorns and berries. Those places were

The men in black—Dennis Huth and Wayne Auton—are shown here in their customary attire prior to a 1996 NASCAR Craftsman Truck Series race at Phoenix. Huth fueled the early growth of the division while Auton has guided it since mid-1995. *High Sierra*

A 10th-place finish in the season-ending CarQuest 420K
earned Ron Hornaday Jr. the
1996 NASCAR Craftsman Truck
Series Championship and a
champagne bath from team
owner Dale Earnhardt during
the title celebration afterward.
High Sierra

Michael Waltrip's MW Windows Ford is at the head of pit road during the half-time break in the 1996 Vegas truck series race. By the end of the second season, the viability of the unique race format, which brought the trucks to pit road for 10 minutes midway through an event, was starting to be questioned by NASCAR, racers, and fans alike. *High Sierra*

Here's a closeup look at Ernie Irvan's 1996 NASCAR Craftsman Truck Series entry. The No. 28 Ford F-150 shows how the bodies of the truck were already taking aerodynamic cues over the original, boxy trucks. This is especially evident in the rounded nose and roof areas of Irvan's F-150, easily the most aerodynamic of the Ford, Chevy, and Dodge brands at the time. The back tailgate now features a bumper reveal as opposed to the flat models of the original 1994 and 1995 trucks and the sides of the truck are flat or "slabbed" as opposed to the rounded and contoured rocker panels on the sides of the initial models. *High Sierra*

awesome. So were I-70 and Colorado National. . . . I wish the crowds could support it enough to where we could go back to places like that."

The short-track era of the NASCAR Craftsman Truck Series was over after just two seasons. The division was firmly established in the American sports landscape, long outdistancing its perceived startup rivals of the WNBA and major league soccer as a viable form of entertainment and marketing tool.

More important, the division was standing shoulder to shoulder with other new, rival racing series like the IRL while far exceeding the television coverage that other rival series like ARCA and ASA received.

The NASCAR Craftsman Truck Series was going to make it. There was no doubt about that. It was time for bigger things at superfast mega tracks like Texas Motor Speedway and California Speedway.

By 1997, the physical shape of the trucks began to change significantly as the division started to make the switch from short tracks to more superspeedway events. Pictured here are the new 1997 truck noses on the Dodge driven by Jimmy Hensley, the Ford driven by Mike Bliss, and the Chevrolet driven by Dave Rezendes. *Nigel Kinrade*

CHAPTER 4

Hitting the Big Time

The 1997 NASCAR Craftsman Truck Series schedule totaled 10 races on tracks a mile or more in length, with three of the events on the superspeedways at Texas, Las Vegas, and California. Because the speeds had increased, the race vehicles began to take on a different configuration as their shape was redefined by the aerodynamic challenges posed by the super-speedway races. The boxy shape of the trucks in 1995 and 1996 quickly morphed into a much sleeker, aero-enhanced version.

"Once you go [to the superspeedways], everything changes," NASCAR Craftsman Truck Series director Wayne Auton said. "You have to make sure you have parity so each make has an opportunity to win. The hardest part was knowing [that] we were going to cost the teams money because we had to have templates."

"The trucks turned out to be a lot different now than when we first started and that really got going in 1997 and 1998," said driver Mike Bliss, who wheeled Jim Smith's No. 2 Team ASE entry those seasons. "We didn't have any downforce on the front of the trucks back then, and in fact, they actually had a little lift. When we started going to the bigger tracks, the trucks really changed. They got a lot sleeker and the balance completely changed. Now we're just sucked to the racetrack. Now we're pretty much wide open at a lot of these tracks like Texas, Charlotte, and Atlanta. I'm not saying it isn't fun, but it's different. The trucks

Jay Sauter was more than happy to slide into the seat of the No. 3 Richard Childress Racing Chevrolet for the 1997 season after Mike Skinner made the jump to the NASCAR NEXTEL Cup Series ranks. *Nigel Kinrade*

According to Wayne Auton, NASCAR Craftsman Truck Series director, the move to the superspeedways made it "twice as hard to enforce the rules" when the trucks were put through technical inspections. Here, the Chevy driven by Rick Carelli gets the once over from a pack of NASCAR officials. Note the more rounded speedway-style nose, a big departure from the flat-front model the Chevys used the year before. *Nigel Kinrade*

are so much better; they've come a long way and that started in 1997."

The first real test of the division's new superspeedway package came at Texas in June where Bliss cracked off a stunning 175.667 mile per hour lap to win the pole. Kenny Irwin held off Boris Said, Rick Crawford, Chuck Bown, and Bliss for his second win of the season in a safe, high-speed race that once and for all silenced any doubts about whether the trucks could compete on the big tracks.

"The trucks were scary fast," Bliss said. "We were trying a lot of different stuff, but nobody really knew what they were doing. There was a lot of trial and effort."

Led by series technical director Chuck Romeo, Huth, and Auton, the NASCAR brain trust consistently massaged the rules to make the division safer and equally competitive between those teams with NASCAR NEXTEL Cup ties and bigger budgets and smaller operations.

In the end, it was Jack Sprague and Rich Bickle—each with three wins—who fought for the 1997 NASCAR Craftsman Truck Series title.

Over the final 10 races, Sprague scored 242 more points than Bickle to win the title by 232

Joe Ruttman made his NASCAR NEXTEL Cup Series debut at Riverside, California, in 1963 and had more than 200 career NASCAR NEXTEL Cup starts by the time he slid behind the wheel of the No. 80 Jack Roush–owned Ford for the 1997 NASCAR Craftsman Truck Series season. Ruttman, who won two races in the division's inaugural 1995 campaign, won the first race on the 1997 schedule at Orlando, Florida. *Nigel Kinrade*

markers, still the largest margin of victory in the history of the NASCAR Craftsman Truck Series.

Ron Hornaday Jr. eventually won the most races in 1997, scoring seven victories, including a stunning performance in June when he led all 200 laps at Bristol.

Joe Ruttman also saw his share of Victory Lane by delivering five wins in the No. 80 Jack Roush entry. Meanwhile, Kenny Irwin, Mike Bliss, Jay Sauter, Bob Keselowski, Ron Fellows, Stacy Compton and Randy Tolsma also won races during the 1997 campaign. Tony Raines closed out the list of winners scoring the first division victory for Dodge.

The 1998 season a new teammate would join Ruttman in the Roush Racing truck camp—eventual division Raybestos Rookie of the Year Greg Biffle.

Both would have strong years, but it was Hornaday and Sprague who claimed 11 of the 27 available wins and finished 1-2 in the championship point standings. Hornaday won six

Continued on page 69

So Long, Thanks for Coming

The NASCAR Craftsman Truck Series' half-time break, which divided the races into two equal segments and allowed teams to make repairs and adjustments without a sophisticated pit crew, was one feature of the series' early years that eventually fell to the wayside.

Initially, the 10-minute break in the action worked just fine, but by the 1998 season, the series had graduated to larger facilities and many of the original factors critical to staging the half-time break were no longer relevant. So after 82 division races, the NASCAR Craftsman Truck Series staged its first live pit stops in the Tempus Resorts 300K at Pikes Peak International Raceway on July 25.

"The half-time break rule was one we really didn't have any choice in making," former NASCAR Craftsman Truck Series director Dennis Huth said. "Because most of the races were contested on short tracks, a lot of those facilities had physical restrictions that wouldn't allow pit stops. Many of them didn't have pit roads and the tracks just weren't conducive to having full-blown pit stops. That's how we came up with the half-time break rule."

Brian France noted that the problem could have been solved in other ways—using a yellow flag to give teams ample time to pit for example—but NASCAR officials thought the half-time break could add suspense to the race.

Doug George's crew scrambles to make repairs to the battered No. 21 Ortho Ford during the half-time break during an event at Tucson Raceway Park in 1996. The 10-minute intermission was a staple of the series in its early years in part because of the physical layout of the small tracks the division used. It also provided the television audience of the new division a chance to hear driver and crew interviews during the race—a unique concept at the time. *High Sierra*

"The idea was that after you came out of an extended break, people who weren't running well could have worked on their trucks and had them running better," he said.

Not everyone thought the competition-based rule was a good idea, though.

"When a half-time break was suggested, I was initially opposed to having it because I felt it wasn't a true motorsports event," Huth said. "It was kind of a made-for-TV showtime event. I have to give Brian [France] a lot of credit because he was the

Rich Bickle's Cummins Dodge crew and Mike Bliss' Team ASE Ford unit were on full tilt in an effort to service their trucks during this half-time break at Mesa Marin in 1996. The half-time break concept allowed teams to make multiple changes to their vehicles—just about everything was open to adjustment or replacement with the exception of the engine—in an effort to make the truck more competitive in the second half of the race. Note that none of the over-the-wall pit crewmembers are wearing helmets, as that was not a rule at the time. *High Sierra*

one that realized we could treat the half-time break like the half-time of a football game. We could let TV [crews] go in and do interviews with the drivers and crew members, let the audience know from a firsthand perspective what happened during the first half of the race, what was wrong with the trucks, and what to expect in the second half of the race. That was very unique and an exciting addition to motorsports television at the time."

The race procedure did eventually catch on and the ability to interview the drivers during a race did provide a novel angle. Remember, the half-time break was a part of the 1995 to 1998 seasons—a period when the advanced TV booth/driver communications that are now a part of NASCAR life were pretty much nonexistent.

"The teams also liked the half-time break rule because it kept costs down," Huth added. "Instead of bringing 10 to 20 guys to the racetrack each weekend like NASCAR NEXTEL Cup and NASCAR Busch Series teams did, they could come with three, four, or five guys. I remember some teams in the early days coming with just the driver and a mechanic."

The days of a single driver and crewman hardly lasted through the first season, however, as teams started to grow in size as the division advanced the schedule into bigger, more

accommodating speedways with ample pit road facilities.

"As the concept of the NASCAR Craftsman Truck Series grew, we realized we could take the trucks wherever we wanted to take them—small or large tracks," Huth said. "We realized the fans wanted actual pit stops, so we started moving to tracks that had the facilities to allow pit stops to happen."

The move paid immediate dividends. Along with new, better driving talent in the series, the division had a record number of drivers visit Victory Lane in 1998—14 in all. Getting rid of the half-time break also legitimized the series as a true racing event in the eyes of some. To others, the rules changes were just a natural evolution process for the division.

"We went from no pit stops and half-time breaks to pit stops in 1998," current NASCAR Craftsman Truck Series director Wayne Auton said. "Then we went from two tires a caution to four tires a caution. We eventually changed the 9:1 engine compression rule to the concept we have today. All of these things were growing steps for the truck series to get where it is today. If you're going to be a national series and be recognized, you have to go with the times."

Ultimately, it was Brian France, the half-time break's greatest proponent, to pass judgment on the concept. He saw it as a way to distinguish the truck events from NASCAR NEXTEL Cup Series and NASCAR Busch Series races, but eventually he realized that the break's time had come and gone.

"Most people believed it actually hurt the credibility of the series a little bit," he said. "People didn't like auto racing having breaks."

Jack Sprague (No. 24), Terry Cook (No. 88), Joe Ruttman (No. 99), and Randy Tolsma (No. 61) were at the head of pit road when the NASCAR Craftsman Truck Series staged its first live pit stops at Pikes Peak International Raceway on July 25, 1998. *High Sierra*

Above and right:
John Nemechek competed in the first NASCAR Craftsman Truck Series race at Phoenix in 1995 and made 43 career division starts before losing his life five days after a crashing on Lap 143 in the March 16, 1997, event at Homestead, Florida. *High Sierra*

Far right:
Rich Bickle's move to the seat of the Darrell Waltrip No. 17 Chevy produced three wins in 1997, including back-to-back poles and victories at Portland and Evergreen early in the season. *Nigel Kinrade*

Continued from page 65

times, including the season-opening race at Orlando, while Sprague racked up 16 top-five finishes that year as Chevrolet won its fourth manufacturer's championship in a many seasons.

"After you win a championship, you know you can do it again," Hornaday said. "You just have to have everything clicking. The competition level is so tough. To do it twice was an unbelievable accomplishment for me."

While there were plenty of other favorite moments for the NASCAR Craftsman Truck Series in 1998, there was an underlying current that the division had lost some of its initial momentum.

Sprague and Hornaday Jr. still had their epic battles on the track, but neither was a new "young gun" media-savvy driver that could carry the series to the public like those the fans were starting to see in the NASCAR NEXTEL Cup ranks.

Additionally, what once was a grassroots, short-track series was now racing more and

It took Dodge 31 races to score its first win after returning to NASCAR as a supporting manufacturer of the series in 1996. Tony Raines did the trick for the manufacturer by steering the No. 19 Kurt Roehrig Pennzoil Mopar to a win at I-70 Speedway on May 24, 1997. Raines dominated the event by leading 149 of 200 laps. *Nigel Kinrade*

more on the superspeedways. Rules changes, like the abandonment of the half-time break, changed the already solid competition for the better, but continuous tinkering of the vehicle and race procedure rules had grown tedious to fans who could see a NASCAR NEXTEL Cup or NASCAR Busch Series event on a super-speedway almost any weekend.

The movement of the trucks to those venues confused and alienated many of the division's initials fans who loved the beatin' and bangin' of the old grassroots short-track days.

"Looking back, if anything, we could have been a little more patient about that," Brian France said in reference to moving the division to the bigger superspeedway venues. "We always use the litmus test of if you can draw 50,000 people—which is a lot of people to an auto race—and do a reasonably good television number and do that consistently, you have a pretty good motorsports property. If anything, I think we

should have been a little more patient as to how long it takes to get to those kind of numbers and we probably were a little anxious."

Despite the angst, the movement of the division to bigger race tracks continued in 1999 with more than half of the 25 series races on ovals of one-mile or more in length. Meanwhile, Portland and Flemington became the latest short-track casualties on the schedule.

But the division—a hit in the boondocks—wasn't playing as well as hoped at some of the bigger venues and was in need of a boost. It would get that and more in 2000 when the NASCAR Craftsman Truck Series would compete at the king of all tracks: Daytona International Speedway.

"It was my dream to get the [NASCAR Craftsman] Truck Series to Daytona," Dennis Huth said. "Most people think that because I was a short-track guy I wasn't interested in having the truck series on the big tracks. That's not true. I

Defending series champion Ron Hornaday Jr. and his Chevrolet sported a special gold paint scheme at several 1997 events. Hornaday was the series leader in wins with seven in 1997, but could only manage a fifth in the final season point standings. *Nigel Kinrade*

supported the move to the big tracks, but I especially wanted to see them run at Daytona."

Rumblings about the division heading to the mecca of stock car racing pinballed around the garage area throughout the 1999 season. Not all the attention was on the Daytona rumor, however, as Sprague, Biffle and Dennis Setzer put on an epic battle for the series championship, with Sprague eventually pulling out his second championship.

Biffle, a winner of a record nine races in 1999, missed the championship by eight points thanks in large part to a seventh-place finish in the final race at California. He also scored his first victory in the division at Michigan in July. His win at Las Vegas in September brought

Ford its first manufacturer's title in the series.

Hornaday Jr. also had a solid year winning the division's 100th race at Evergreen Speedway in May earning a $100,000 bonus from Craftsman for the achievement in the landmark event. He also became the first driver to win an event in all five years of the series when he captured the Chevy Trucks 150 at Phoenix in March.

Modified racer Mike Stefanik and late-model pilot Scott Hansen battled for Raybestos Rookie of the Year honors with Stefanik taking the title by 25 points.

Still, hardly anyone was focused on the present as garage conversations were all about the start of the 2000 season at Daytona. That was what everyone was shooting for.

After teaming up to win their first race together at North Wilkesboro in 1995, Mike Bliss and Barry Dodson led the truck series with six poles—including three in a row at Mesa Marin, California, and Phoenix—late in the 1997 season. The team's only win came from the front-row starting spot at California, where Bliss led all but seven of the 100 laps. *Nigel Kinrade*

Rich Bickle leads Ernie Irvan and Mike Bliss through the corner at Martinsville in September. Bickle went on to win his third and final event of the season, all of them coming from the pole and on short tracks. *Nigel Kinrade*

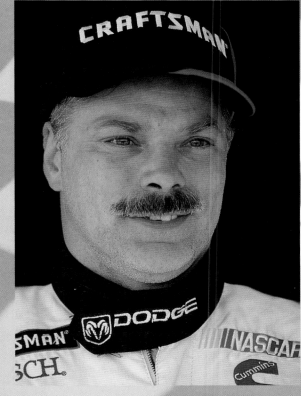

The 1997 NASCAR Craftsman Truck Series season produced a number of first-time winners, including *(above left)* Ken Irwin at Homestead; *(above right)* Randy Tolsma at Mesa Marin; and *(left)* Bob Keselowski at Richmond. *Nigel Kinrade*

The battle for the 1997 NASCAR Craftsman Truck Series title came down to Jack Sprague and Rich Bickle, with Sprague putting on a late-season charge to take the crown. Sprague never finished out of the top 10 and had a 4.6 finishing average over the final 10 races of the season to win the title by 232 points. *Nigel Kinrade*

It was an all-Ford front row as polesitter Mike Bliss (No. 2) and Bryan Reffner (No. 66) brought the 36-truck field to the start of the 1997 GM Goodwrench/Delco 300 at Phoenix International Raceway. Neither driver figured in the winning outcome, as Joe Ruttman closed out the season with back-to-back victories at Phoenix and Las Vegas. *Nigel Kinrade*

Jack Sprague used the power of Hendrick Motorsports to propel himself to the 1997 NASCAR Craftsman Truck Series championship and a career in the division that now spans a decade and a total of three division championships. *Nigel Kinrade*

Richmond International Raceway was aglow as the NASCAR Craftsman Truck Series invaded the Virginia oval for a night race in September. Jack Sprague won the event by 0.299 of a second over Ernie Irvan, Greg Biffle, Joe Ruttman, and Butch Miller. *Nigel Kinrade*

Ron Hornaday Jr. got off to a fast start, winning the first race of the 1998 NASCAR Craftsman Truck Series season at Orlando. The victory was his 18th in just 71 career division starts at the time. Hornaday eventually won six races in 1998 while en route to his second NASCAR Craftsman Truck Series championship. *Nigel Kinrade*

Far right:

Tammy Jo Kirk made 32 career NASCAR Craftsman Truck Series starts over the 1997 and 1998 seasons. A former late-model driver who won some of that division's biggest races, Kirk had her best 1998 finish at Bristol where she started 28th and finished 13th. Kirk was a nationally licensed flat track motorcyclist and the first female to compete in the series. *Nigel Kinrade*

David Starr made his NASCAR Craftsman Truck Series debut in the third race of the 1998 season at Phoenix, starting last in the No. 49 Rehrer/Morrison Chevy and finishing 25th. Starr competed in five 1998 series events. His best finish was at Texas in June, where he placed 18th. *Nigel Kinrade*

Greg Biffle made the jump from the West Coast late-model stock car ranks to the NASCAR Craftsman Truck Series in 1998 and scored eight top-5 finishes while en route to an eighth-place finish in the final season point standings and the division's Raybestos Rookie of the Year award. Biffle debuted at Walt Disney World Speedway in Orlando in the No. 80 Roush Racing Ford, finishing fifth in the season-opening event. It was the only time Biffle ran the No. 80 all year, as he switched to the No. 50 after that. *Nigel Kinrade*

Nearly every hood was open wide as teams prepared their trucks prior to a 1998 NASCAR Craftsman Truck Series event. While everyone points to the number of drivers who got their big break during the early years of the division, hundreds of crewmembers also found their way to the big time world of NASCAR thanks to the series. *Nigel Kinrade*

Far right:
After running four races in 1997, Andy Houston joined the NASCAR Craftsman Truck Series on a full-time basis in 1998 and earned his first division victory at New Hampshire International Speedway on August 2. Houston posted nine top-10 finishes in the No. 60 Addington Racing Chevrolet, narrowly missing out on the Raybestos Rookie of the Year title to Greg Biffle. *Nigel Kinrade*

Normally a trusty friend thanks to its lower 9:1 compression rating, this engine sits alone after failing during a 1998 truck series practice session. The 9:1 engine configuration—which had relatively few failures during the early years of the truck series—was dropped prior to the 2001 season in favor of a 12:1 compression model. *Nigel Kinrade*

Terry Cook broke into the truck series in 1996 and won for the first time in his 34th career start, capturing the Stevens Beil 200 at Flemington Speedway on August 8, 1998. Cook, in the PBA Tour Chevrolet, beat Ron Hornaday Jr. to the checkered flag by 1.624 seconds. *Nigel Kinrade*

After winning at Mesa Marin late in the 1997 season, Randy Tolsma got a full-time opportunity in the NASCAR Craftsman Truck Series in 1998, behind the wheel of the No. 61 IWX Motor Freight Chevy. Here Tolsma, a former open-wheel ace, battles Ron Hornaday Jr. at Phoenix. Tolsma suffered an engine failure on Lap 111 and finished 34th. *Nigel Kinrade*

Ron Hornaday Jr. became the first driver to repeat as champion by adding the 1998 NASCAR Craftsman Truck Series title to his 1996 crown. He finished in the top 10 in 22 of the 27 events (81 percent) and posted an average finish of 7.2. He also racked up his victory total to 23 in just four truck racing seasons by adding six wins to the mark in 1998. *Nigel Kinrade*

Greg Biffle (No. 50) and Mike Bliss (No. 2) lead the field to the green flag at the start of the 1998 NAPA 250 at Martinsville Speedway. Biffle's pole win was his third straight. He also made top qualifying runs at Memphis Motorsports Park and Gateway International Raceway near St. Louis. Biffle finished eighth in the Martinsville event while Bliss came home 13th. *Nigel Kinrade*

It was bumper-to-tailgate action as Randy Tolsma (No. 25), Jack Sprague (No. 24), and Jimmy Hensley (No. 43) wheeled their way through Turn One at Martinsville in April. This kind of short-track action was at a premium in 1999 as only nine of the 25 events were held on half-mile ovals that season. *Nigel Kinrade*

Ron Hornaday Jr. began the defense of his 1998 NASCAR Craftsman Truck Series championship by winning two of the first three races of the 1999 season. The victories proved to be the only two triumphs of the year for the then 41-year-old driver, as he fell to seventh in the final 1999 championship standings. *Nigel Kinrade*

It didn't take long for the NASCAR Craftsman Truck Series to get used to live pit stops after ditching the half-time break concept midway through the 1998 season. Here, Greg Biffle, a winner of a record nine series events in 1999, is at the head of the field as he pits for fresh tires and fuel at Martinsville.
Nigel Kinrade

Jimmy Hensley gave Dodge its first win of the 1999 season when he captured the NAPA 250 at Martinsville. Hensley, one of the most respected drivers to ever compete in the series, finished his career with two wins, four poles, and 27 top-5 finishes in 146 division starts. *Nigel Kinrade*

Mike Wallace jumped from Ken Schrader's Chevy to Jim Smith's Team ASE Ford in 1999 and produced immediate results by winning two races, including the season-opening event at Homestead-Miami Speedway. Wallace posted a 10.3 finishing average in 1999 while en route to a sixth-place effort in the season standings. *Nigel Kinrade*

Mike Stefanik opened the 1999 season with a bang, finishing second in the season-opening event at Homestead-Miami Speedway. The effort proved to be his best finish of the season and his only top-10 finish of the 1999 NASCAR Craftsman Truck Series campaign, but those totals were still good enough to give the driver of the No. 66 Carlin Oil Burners Ford the division's Raybestos Rookie of the Year title. *Nigel Kinrade*

Jack Sprague took home the big hardware and a check for more than $834,000 at the season-ending NASCAR Craftsman Truck Series banquet held at the Fairmont Hotel in San Francisco. It was the second series championship he won. He earned the title by a mere eight points over Greg Biffle. *High Sierra*

A little over five years after the first NASCAR Craftsman Truck Series exhibition race at Bakersfield, California, the trucks were poised to stage their first race at Daytona International Speedway. Several trucks were tested at the 2.5-mile Florida oval for the first time on September 13, 1999, in preparation for the announced 2000 season-opening event. *Nigel Kinrade*

Joe Ruttman (No. 18) and Mike Wallace (No. 2) take the green flag as the field rumbles through the tri-oval at Daytona International Speedway in the first Daytona 250 NASCAR Craftsman Truck Series race on February 18, 2000. Wallace eventually captured the checkered flag in the event, finishing ahead of series rookie Kurt Busch, Andy Houston, Terry Cook, and Kenny Martin. *High Sierra*

CHAPTER 5

Daytona Destiny

Like Indianapolis and LeMans, the mere mention of Daytona immediately brings auto racing to mind. Long before Bill France Sr. and a group of businessmen founded NASCAR in 1947, Daytona was famous for its land-speed record runs and stock car races along its silky smooth sand beaches.

France's dream raceway–Daytona International Speedway–started to become a reality in 1957 when he signed a lease with the Daytona Beach Racing and Recreation Facilities District for 500 acres of cypress swamp land near the old World War II naval station west of the city. Seed money for the project was a mere $35,000.

France envisioned a track that would rival Indianapolis, and he proposed a 2.5-mile, 31-degree banked, D-shaped oval unlike any other facility in motorsports at the time. In 1959, France finished the project at an estimated final cost of $1.6 million. Since then, Daytona International Speedway has come to be recognized as one of the greatest landmarks in the world of motorsports.

In 2000–40 years after Daytona International Speedway opened–the NASCAR Craftsman Truck Series was preparing for its first event at the track. There were many questions concerning the suitability of the trucks racing

Experience paid off for veteran NASCAR NEXTEL Cup Series driver Joe Ruttman as he won the pole position for the first NASCAR Craftsman Truck Series race at Daytona. Ruttman wound up 19th in the race when the engine expired in his Bobby Hamilton–owned Dodge on Lap 64.

Winning the Big One

Mike Wallace's victory in the first NASCAR Craftsman Truck Series race at Daytona featured a final-lap scramble that made the event one of the most memorable races at the legendary track in recent years.

Here is Wallace's account of that final critical lap of the inaugural Daytona 250 at Daytona International Speedway in 2000, one of the series' most defining races:

"Andy Houston and I were racing back and forth the whole last part of the race. We were swapping the lead back and forth a couple times a lap. I was leading when we came to the start/finish line to take the white flag, and by the time we got to Turn One, I was sixth. I had gotten shuffled back and all I could think of was that I had led most of this race and now it was slipping away from me on the last lap.

"I was depressed, disappointed, and a few other words I can't mention to go along with that. I had led somewhere around 60 to 65 laps of a 100-lap race and now it was all going down the drain on the final lap.

"I remember seeing Andy get out in front of the group by quite a ways, and I knew from my previous speedway experience that he didn't need to be doing that. He needed to be back with the pack. Everyone lined up with Andy as we hit the back straight, which is what usually happens when someone sees a guy making a dominant move. That's what you do in restrictor-plate racing. But with the trucks I knew that if I could get a push from someone, I'd be able to draft back up to them. If I could do that, maybe I still had a chance to win.

"Going down the back straight, I felt this incredible push and I looked in my mirror to see Ken Martin in the No. 98 truck stuck up my back bumper. I started to pick up speed and the draft from the lead group and I knew that when I got to Turn Three, I was going to go to the top of the racetrack. I could feel the push Ken was giving me and I knew I could clear the trucks in front of me if I went to the outside. I was going up there come hell or high water. Whatever was going to happen was going to happen.

"We got to Turn Three, and I went to the top of the racetrack. I got on the outside of Andy and he twitched

Mike Wallace was all smiles as he emerged from the Team ASE Ford after winning the inaugural Daytona 250 at Daytona International Speedway. Wallace went on to win at Mesa Marin Raceway later in 2000—his only other victory of the season and the most recent of his four career NASCAR Craftsman Truck Series triumphs. *High Sierra*

just a little bit. I felt bad that I left Ken on the bottom, but thank goodness he was there. I could have never won that race without him.

"Coming off of Turn Four, I was able to drive back past Andy and win the race. It was an unbelievable event. Everyone was so excited. It was an incredible scene.

"I've told numerous people over the years that there will always be other Daytona truck series winners, but there will never be another inaugural NASCAR Craftsman

Truck Series race winner at Daytona. There were so many people that thought the truck race at Daytona was going to be a big failure. They said it was stupid to have [trucks] running 190 miles an hour there. We were hearing that all winter.

"That race will probably always be my biggest win because it had so much attention attached to it. Sure, some people will remember (Geoffrey) Bodine's big wreck, but more remember what a great race it was."

The inaugural NASCAR Craftsman Truck Series race at Daytona International Speedway will forever be remembered for one of the most violent accidents in the history of the track. It began when Geoffrey Bodine (No. 15) tangled with Dennis Setzer (No. 46), sending Bodine climbing over the truck of Lyndon Amick (No. 52) and into the fence. Bodine's truck then starts to tumble as Kurt Busch (No. 99) races by. Eventually, Bodine's truck erupted into a ball of fire before coming to a rest just past the Daytona trioval. Bodine—the 1986 Daytona 500 champion—recovered from his injuries to race again. *High Sierra*

on the big track: Could the larger, boxy trucks compete side-by-side at nearly 200 miles per hour? Could the drivers handle the ultrafast Daytona Superspeedway speeds? Would the trucks have to be equipped with carburetor restrictor plates to slow them down like their NASCAR NEXTEL Cup and Busch Series counterparts?

Perhaps the most important question was if the trucks could stay on the ground.

Mike Wallace (center) is flanked on the right by team owner and NASCAR Craftsman Truck Series pioneer Jim Smith and surrounded by the rest of his Ultra Motorsports team as they celebrate in Victory Lane after winning the 2000 Daytona 250. Wallace, driving the Team ASE Ford, averaged 130.152 miles per hour in capturing the event that was slowed six times for 25 caution laps. He earned $80,099 for the victory. *High Sierra*

Many of those questions were quickly answered during preseason testing. Despite their less-than-sleek shape, the trucks were stable in the draft and ran surprising well on the high-speed track. NASCAR even decided to allow the trucks to run without restrictor plates to give them more throttle response. The slingshot—a move from the pre-restrictor plate days at Daytona where a driver uses the clean air from the vehicle in front of them to help execute a pass—was suddenly back in NASCAR racing.

"The most awe-inspiring thing I remember from the first NASCAR Craftsman Truck Series test at Daytona was that the trucks drafted so well," driver Mike Wallace said. "The closing rates were so great. We had heard all the stories from yesteryear about the draft and how it worked, but even though I had raced at Daytona and Talladega before in the NASCAR NEXTEL Cup Series, [NASCAR] Busch Series, and ARCA series, I had never experienced anything like what the draft was with the trucks. It was phenomenal.

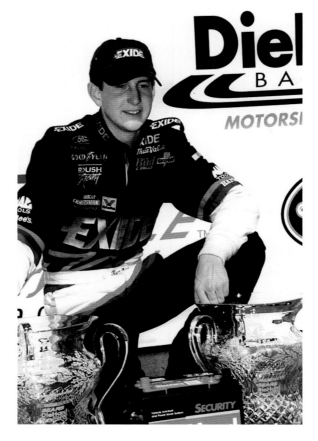

Kurt Busch proved to be the most prolific rookie in the history of the NASCAR Craftsman Truck Series by scoring a freshman record of four wins in 2000. Busch, shown here after his first truck series win at Milwaukee and pitting his No. 99 Roush Ford at Dover, finished second in the final season standings—still the best finish for a rookie driver in the series championship standings.
High Sierra

Roush Racing featured a potent one-two punch in 2000 with Greg Biffle (No. 50) and rookie Kurt Busch (No. 99) behind the wheel of twin Ford F-150s. Here, Busch pulls up to congratulate Biffle after they finished first and second at Pikes Peak in May. The victory was the first of five wins that season for Biffle. *High Sierra*

You could run wide open, but even if you did have to lift out of the gas, you could recover."

Yet, the question of whether the trucks would stay on the ground in a crash situation was still up for grabs.

"The trucks were more aerodynamic going backward than forward," said Wayne Auton, the current NASCAR Craftsman Truck Series director. "We had to really get on top of our game to not have to go there without restrictor plates. We did everything we could to stay away from that. That was the hardest part of getting the trucks ready to race at Daytona. That, along with not knowing what was going to happen by the end of the checkered flag."

When the gates swung open for the 2000 Daytona Speedweeks, 52 drivers and their trucks were on hand to attempt to qualify for the inaugural Daytona 250. Experience on the big track proved to be valuable as 55-year-old driver Joe Ruttman—a veteran of 19 Daytona NASCAR NEXTEL Cup Series starts—won the pole with a lap of 187.563 miles per hour in the No. 18 Dana Dodge.

Ruttman, and fellow front-row starter Wallace, led the 36-truck field under the green flag on Friday, February 18. It didn't take long for the fireworks to start as a six-truck melee in Turn Two brought out the first caution of the day. That incident, however, paled in comparison to the wreck that would occur on Lap 56.

Racing in a pack through the trioval, Geoffrey Bodine's mount went airborne into the front stretch catch fence after contact with another truck. The fence shredded Bodine's truck as the vehicle bucked and tumbled down the track amid a huge fireball. The trucks of Jimmy Hensley, Kurt Busch, Jamie McMurray, Lonnie Rush Jr., John Young, Rob Morgan, Jimmy Kitchens, Lyndon Amick, Rick Carelli, B. A. Wilson, Lance Norick, and Terry Cook were also swept up into the mishap and the race had to be red-flagged.

Greg Biffle dominated the 2000 NASCAR Craftsman Truck Series championship chase, clinching the title with one race remaining in the 24-event season. Despite leaving the race after a Lap 79 accident and finishing 25th in the O'Reilly 400 at Texas Motor Speedway, Biffle and his crew were able to celebrate the championship thanks to a 250-point lead heading into the final race at California. Biffle later celebrated in style, posing in a tux with his truck and the championship trophy prior to the season-ending banquet in Phoenix. *High Sierra*

Bodine was immediately transported to nearby Halifax Medical Center in Daytona with serious injuries, but he eventually recovered.

Meanwhile, the Daytona infield care center looked like a triage unit in a war zone as Hensley, Rush, Amick, and others were checked out and released after the incident.

After an extended cleanup period, the race went back to green flag conditions where Wallace and Andy Houston staged a furious battle for the win, swapping the lead nine times over the final 42 laps.

Eventually, Wallace, driving the Team ASE Ford, powered into the lead on the final lap, and he took the win by 0.237 of a second in front of Busch, Houston, Cook, and Kenny Martin.

"We built a fast truck," Wallace said. "At that time, the rules were a little bit more liberal and we built the narrowest little Ford truck we could. They didn't have any minimum width rules for the body panels at that time. They had a front nose and valence width, but the sides of the body, the doors, the rear of the truck, and the bumper cover all didn't have to be a certain width. We did a lot of work that was very much well within the rules. We had a creative team, and when it came time to go to Daytona, we were able to take advantage of that. We had guys that could take existing parts and modify them to fit within the rulebook."

"There are a lot of things that make a car or truck fast on a superspeedway," Wallace added. "Once we knew we were going to Daytona, the effort we put into having the best truck body, chassis- and motor-wise, was incredible. There's no doubt that effort allowed us to have a little bit of a competitive advantage. There were other people who were doing it too. Maybe not all the field, but the best teams were."

Wallace's truck was fittingly owned by one of the four series founders, Jim Smith.

"I remember telling Jim Smith on the radio as we were coming to the green flag that he had a lot to do with the NASCAR Craftsman Truck Series coming to fruition originally and he should be proud to see it now at Daytona," Wallace said. "I said, 'Okay, Smith, here you are—from the desert to Daytona.' "

Smith admits that he had mixed feelings when NASCAR truck racing started moving away from the short tracks and hitting the superspeedways, but he knew racing at Daytona would only raise the profile of the series.

"There was no way you could argue that and seeing the trucks race at Daytona was one of the greatest accomplishments of my life," he said. "That was especially true when my truck won the inaugural race there. That was one of my greatest days in racing and something I will never forget. Daytona is the kind of place that if you win a dog race there, it's memorable."

Ironically, while Bodine's crash was and still is considered one of the most spectacular in the history of the speedway, most of the talk after the race was how well the trucks competed on the giant oval. In fact, many of the same people who doubted the ability to race pickup trucks at Daytona were now saying the division put on the best show of the 2000 Speedweeks racing calendar. Additionally, the inaugural Daytona 250, with its spectacular on track action, brought a whole new legion of fans to the truck series.

"Aside from the horrific wreck that Geoff Bodine had, the first NASCAR Craftsman Truck Series race was one of the best races at Daytona in years," Wallace said. "After the first Daytona race, a lot of people who had dismissed the series as just a bunch of short-track racers took notice that it was a great series with some incredible racing."

After competing in 12 NASCAR Craftsman Truck Series races in 2000, Coy Gibbs decided to take on the entire 2001 series schedule. Gibbs, son of NFL Hall of Fame coach and NASCAR team owner Joe Gibbs, eventually finished 10th in the 2000 series championship standings, scoring two top-5 finishes and seven top-10 finishes that season. Gibbs now is an assistant coach under his father with the Washington Redskins. *Nigel Kinrade*

The division rode the momentum of the Daytona race, new fan interest, and industry acceptance throughout the rest of the 2000 season. Greg Biffle, winner of a division-high nine races in 1999, won five races while en route to the 2000 title, beating his Roush Racing teammate Kurt Busch for the championship by a whopping 230 points (3,826 to 3,596).

Busch, meanwhile, easily captured the 2000 Raybestos Rookie of the Year award by winning an unprecedented four races—still a record for first-year drivers in the truck series.

Despite these accomplishments, any recollections of the 2000 season begin and end with the inaugural Daytona race.

"I thought the Daytona race would do what it was supposed to do, which was to showcase the guys during Speedweeks," Brian France said. "The racing ended up being better than we could have hoped for. That race continues to be one of the best of Speedweeks every year."

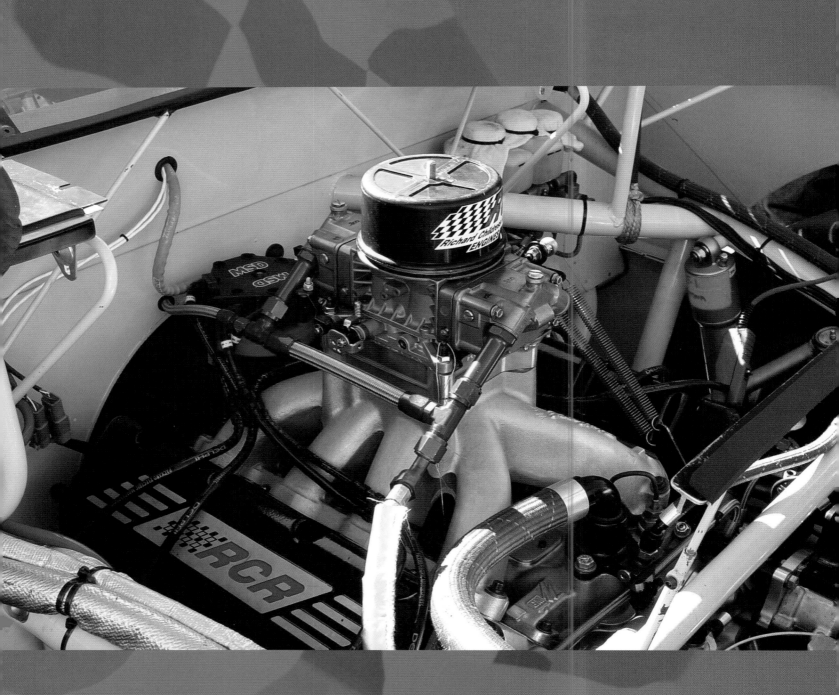

One of the biggest technical changes in the series came in 2001 when the division replaced the 9:1 compression engine with the more powerful 12:1 compression model. The current 12:1 configuration—this one produced by Richard Childress Racing for Ron Hornaday Jr.—is pictured here. *John Close*

CHAPTER 6

An Identity Odyssey

As the NASCAR Craftsman Truck Series entered its seventh season in 2001, it was losing some of its hottest stars to the NASCAR NEXTEL Cup Series and NASCAR Busch Series world. Kurt Busch ignited the exodus after final race of the 2000 season at California by announcing in Victory Lane he would move to NASCAR NEXTEL Cup racing for Roush Racing the following season.

Like Busch, Greg Biffle was also on the move in 2001, heading to the NASCAR Busch Series while Andy Houston and Mike Wallace, third and fourth respectively in the final 2000 season point standings, bolted the truck series for the NASCAR NEXTEL Cup Series ranks. Clearly, the division had become a stepping stone for drivers to move up the NASCAR ladder, but the defections left the NASCAR Craftsman Truck Series with a driver identity crunch, especially during the 2001 campaign.

The driver cupboard wasn't completely bare as Jim Smith retooled his Ultra Motorsports team to include two trucks—Scott Riggs in the potent No. 2 and a new team featuring ex-NASCAR NEXTEL Cup Series star Ted Musgrave. Another newcomer, Travis Kvapil,

took over Houston's seat at Addington Racing while a pair of drivers with famous fathers—Coy Gibbs and Ricky Hendrick—joined the series

Longtime NASCAR NEXTEL Cup Series driver Ted Musgrave joined the series ranks in 2001 behind the wheel of the potent No. 1 Mopar Performance Parts Dodge, fielded by Ultra Motorsports. Musgrave proved to be an instant hit, winning a division-high seven races and finishing second in the 2001 championship standings. *Nigel Kinrade*

Scott Riggs got his start in NASCAR by qualifying seventh for his first series start at O'Reilly Raceway Park at Indianapolis in 1999. Two years later, Riggs was behind the wheel of the potent No. 2 Team ASE Dodge and won five times that season. Riggs used his truck success to move on to the NASCAR NEXTEL Cup Series in 2004. *Nigel Kinrade*

full time after running select truck series events in 2000.

For Musgrave, who had competed in 298 NASCAR NEXTEL Cup Series races over the previous decade, the switch to truck racing was a breath of fresh air.

"It was a lot like when I was back in Wisconsin racing ASA, ARTGO, all the short tracks. Racing was fun again," Musgrave said. "I never looked at coming to the NASCAR Craftsman Truck Series as a step down. I looked at coming here as a way to have a lot of fun. It's all about the racing. It's not a big circus; it's about coming here and performing well."

Driver changes weren't the only differences that greeted fans at the start of the 2001 season as the tried-and-true 9:1 compression engine was replaced by the more powerful 12:1 compression model.

"We knew it was going to be expensive, but it was the right thing to do," NASCAR Craftsman Truck Series Director Wayne Auton said. "Our engine programs had stepped up so much that you were either going to run up front or go right to the back of the pack. It made sense to make the switch because there was so much crossover between engine builders in the three national series. If an engine builder can build one specific engine for those three series, the price of the engines will go down. If they were still building 9:1 engines in today's times and you consider how prices have gone up, they'd cost as much as 12:1s do now because of the limited quantity they would be produced in."

Additionally, the schedule continued to morph more toward the bigger tracks as NASCAR's first superspeedway–venerable Darlington Raceway, which opened in 1950– joined Dover Downs International Speedway and the all-new Kansas Speedway on the 2001 NASCAR Craftsman Truck Series slate of events.

Meanwhile, the old-guard short tracks continued to fall off the schedule as Evergreen and the short track at Nashville Fairgrounds succumbed to the march of the big tracks, as did the division's experiment with road course racing with the removal of

Ricky Hendrick was just 20 years old when he opened the 2001 NASCAR Craftsman Truck Series season with a second-place finish at Daytona behind the wheel of his family-owned Hendrick Motorsports Chevrolet. Hendrick posted eight top-5 efforts that season. He also became the youngest race winner in series history when he won the O'Reilly Auto Parts 250 at Kansas Speedway on July 7, 2001. The event was the first time the truck series hosted a race at the track. *Nigel Kinrade/High Sierra*

Jon Wood was one of many young newcomers to the NASCAR Craftsman Truck Series in 2001. Wood made his series debut at Martinsville, where he finished 31st in the Advance Auto Parts 250. In all, Wood, just 19 at the time, made 16 series starts in 2001, scoring top-5 finishes at Kansas and California.
Nigel Kinrade

Scott Riggs gets service on the No. 2 Team ASE Dodge as a packed house looks on during this 2001 event at Dover Downs International Speedway. Big crowds are the rule for the series, especially when races are held as companion events to the NASCAR NEXTEL Cup Series at tracks like Dover.
High Sierra

Watkins Glen and Portland International from the 2001 racing calendar.

About the only place the NASCAR Craftsman Truck Series didn't suffer from an identity crisis heading into the 2001 season was on the television dial, where ESPN and ESPN2 were awarded sole telecasting rights of the series. Previously, the TV package had been an amalgamation of network and cable coverage that for years had left viewers clicking their remotes to find the races each week. Under the new ESPN agreements, all but two of the 24 events would be carried live on the two networks.

Leading the call on the races from the telecast booth was veteran broadcaster Jerry Punch.

"It was like the old days when I first started doing radio for MRN in the late 1970s," Punch said. "The teams were all so close, and they traveled to and from the racetracks together, stayed in the same hotels, ate in the same restaurants. There weren't a lot of motor coaches where people went away to be sequestered in their own

Terry Cook blasts the No. 29 Power Stroke Diesel Ford to the inside of Brian Rose (No. 51) during the 2001 Kroger 200 at Richmond International Raceway. Cook scored 16 top-10 finishes and placed seventh in the final 2001 NASCAR Craftsman Truck Series championship standings. *High Sierra*

Jack Sprague was the last of the remaining original kingpins of the NASCAR Craftsman Truck Series as the division headed into the 2001 season. Sprague made the best of it, rolling to a third championship. Here, Sprague's No. 24 Chevrolet leads Rick Crawford into the turn at Las Vegas. *High Sierra*

South Boston (Virginia) Speedway, a 0.400-mile throwback to the short tracks of the early days of the NASCAR Craftsman Truck Series, was the 20th stop on the 2001 schedule. Ted Musgrave, shown here celebrating in a makeshift Victory Lane with his Ultra Motorsports crew, won the 250-lap, 100-mile race, beating Dennis Setzer, Jack Sprague, Scott Riggs, and Joe Ruttman to the finish. *High Sierra*

little worlds. There were no million-dollar islands. They hung out in their trailers. It was like turning back the clock."

Along with the focused coverage from ESPN, the NASCAR Craftsman Truck Series was breaking into new editorial territory with expanded coverage in industry trade and mainstream print publications. The division had also developed a large following on the internet thanks to websites such as NASCAR.com and TruckSeries.com.

One thing that didn't change in 2001 was seeing Jack Sprague run at the front of the pack. While almost all of the drivers he competed

against early on in the series' beginning had moved on to either the NASCAR Busch Series or NASCAR NEXTEL Cup Series, Sprague stayed firmly entrenched in the trucks behind the wheel of a Hendrick Motorsports Chevy. Armed with backing from new sponsor NetZero in 2001, Sprague won four events and posted 15 top-five finishes en route to capturing a record third division title.

It wasn't a total cakewalk for Sprague as Musgrave dominated Victory Lane with seven wins, finishing second in the final 2001 championship standings. Riggs, Musgrave's Ultra Motorsports teammate, also went to Victory

Jack Sprague cruised to his third NASCAR Craftsman Truck Series championship in 2001, taking new team sponsor NetZero to the top of the standings with him. Sprague finished no worse than fourth in six of the final seven races of the season to capture a record third series title. He is shown here at speed at Las Vegas *(above left)*, celebrating his championship after the final race of the season at California *(left)*, and on the beach in Miami with team owner Rick Hendrick and the 2001 series championship trophy *(above right)*. *High Sierra*

Lane five times and finished fifth in the championship chase to give team owner Smith the most potent one-two punch in NASCAR Craftsman Truck Series history.

"The truck series was a revival for me," said Musgrave, who had come close but was never able to win in the NASCAR NEXTEL Cup Series. "I was in the Cup and Busch series for a long time and it was hard. When I first came to the truck series, it was a little easier. We had really, really good equipment."

Joe Ruttman, meanwhile, notched two wins, including a victory from the pole in the series' second-ever race at Daytona. Unlike the inaugural event, the 2001 Daytona race was a comparatively timid affair with none of the aerobatics that punctuated the 2000 event.

The Raybestos Rookie of the Year battle came down to Kvapil and Hendrick with Kvapil taking the honors on the strength of a late-season charge. Each driver smashed Kurt Busch's mark of 16 top-10 finishes in a season with Hendrick notching 19 and Kvapil 18. Both drivers won a race—Kvapil at Texas and Hendrick at Kansas.

At season's end, the changes that seemed to cloud the identity of the NASCAR Craftsman Truck Series at the beginning of the 2001 campaign were forgotten as the one constant since the inception of the division—great racing—shined brightly through.

"The truck series races were everything I grew up watching," Punch said. "It was slingshots, drafting, beatin', and bangin'. Guys would get out of their trucks and tempers would be flaring. It was like the old days of Richard Petty, David Pearson, and the Allisons. Man, I thought it was great."

With the half-time break rule now just a distant memory, NASCAR Craftsman Truck Series teams were fielding top-notch pit crews by the 2002 season. Here, Jason Leffler's Ultra Motorsports crew springs into action during a pit stop at Martinsville. *Nigel Kinrade*

CHAPTER 7

Stability and Acceptance

The transformation of the NASCAR Craftsman Truck Series from a short-track novelty to an accepted major attraction on the nation's premiere speedways was finally complete by the start of the 2002 season. Past issues like the race schedule and rule and driver changes were no longer seen as earth-shattering events. The division had officially attained major bragging rights as one of NASCAR's "Big Three"—right alongside its NASCAR NEXTEL Cup Series and NASCAR Busch Series counterparts.

Unlike the past, hardly anyone blinked when Jack Sprague—the last of the original hot shots of the NASCAR Craftsman Truck Series— left the division to drive in the NASCAR Busch Series in 2002. The truck series still had established veteran drivers like Ted Musgrave, Dennis Setzer, Robert Pressley, Mike Bliss, Terry Cook, and Rick Crawford to draw from while Jason Leffler and Brendan Gaughan headed the list of talented newcomers to the series.

Pressley, a veteran of more than 200 NASCAR NEXTEL Cup Series career starts, opened the 2002 truck racing season at Daytona by winning the 250-mile race in his first division start. Meanwhile, Bliss, back in the series full time after a failed trip to the NASCAR NEXTEL Cup Series ranks, won a division-high five events on his way to the 2002 NASCAR Craftsman Truck Series title.

"We didn't even know if we were going to race going into the 2002 season," Bliss said. "We almost didn't make it to the first race at Daytona because our team owner, Steve Coulter, didn't think he could afford to go racing. Our team manager, Dave Fuge, didn't have a license with NASCAR at that time and he was trying to get reinstated. It was an uphill

Without a ride for the 2001 season, Mike Bliss returned to the NASCAR Craftsman Truck Series with a vengeance in 2002, winning the division championship. Bliss won five times and scored 18 top-10 finishes in 22 events to notch his first major NASCAR title. *Nigel Kinrade*

Ted Musgrave (No. 1) and Ricky Hendrick (No. 17) lead the field through the trioval at Daytona International Speedway to start the 2001 season. Robert Pressley, a longtime NASCAR NEXTEL Cup Series and NASCAR Busch Series regular, won the Daytona 250 in his first career NASCAR Craftsman Truck Series start. Musgrave, shown during a pit stop at right, settled for second with Brian Rose and Joe Ruttman making it a Dodge sweep of the first four places. *Nigel Kinrade*

fight all year and we certainly never expected to go out and win the championship.

"We did it under the radar and that's what really made it fun," Bliss added. "I think there were some teams that didn't take us seriously. Winning that championship meant a lot to me, to all of us."

While Bliss was basking in the glow of the championship, Gaughan dominated the Raybestos Rookie of the Year chase, taking over the lead in the rookie standings after the third race of the season at Martinsville.

The division got another boost when NASCAR NEXTEL Cup veteran Bobby Hamilton decided he had had his fill of the top NASCAR series' ranks and joined the truck series full time in 2003. Hamilton would have a significant impact on the series, winning two races—Darlington and Miami—as well as finishing sixth in the final point standings.

More importantly, Hamilton, along with former NASCAR NEXTEL Cup Series veterans like Musgrave and Pressley, gave the series further legitimacy as a place where drivers could stay and race, as well as one where they could build their careers.

"I asked Bobby Hamilton why he decided to come to the truck series and he told me 'This is the kind of racing I grew up with,'" Musgrave said. "'It's a place where you can wear your jeans and your T-shirt, hang out at the shop all week, work with your guys, go to the track, practice, qualify, race, go out for a burger, and bench race with your team afterward. This is the way it should be.'"

Another 2003 NASCAR Craftsman Truck Series newcomer, Carl Edwards, also had a profound effect on the division. Just one year removed from placing ads in racing trade papers trying to find a ride, the energetic former Missouri dirt-track racer won three events and the Raybestos Rookie of the Year title.

The bookends for the 2003 NASCAR Craftsman Truck Series season came in the

Pit road was full of action in the 2002 Advance Auto Parts 250 as Terry Cook, Bill Lester, and Carlos Contreras made their final pit stops. In the end, Dennis Setzer celebrated in Victory Lane after he rallied from the 33rd starting position to lead the final 32 laps.
Nigel Kinrade

opening event at Daytona and the division finale at Homestead. At Daytona, Crawford rallied from his 19th starting position to win in a photo finish. He slipped his Ford to the inside of Pressley's Dodge on the last lap and Travis Kvapil joined the battle on the high side as the trio crossed the start/finish line with Crawford taking the three-wide win by a microscopic 0.027 of a second.

"It surprised me to win," Crawford said. "I had gone 120 races without winning and I remember thinking late in the race that a caution or something little was going to take it away from me. You plan things at Daytona in a split second, and at the end, we were three-wide and I was fortunate to win at Daytona. It was an amazing race and an amazing day."

Kvapil used the strong Daytona start to give the IWX Racing team its second-straight championship—the first back-to-back team title in NASCAR Craftsman Truck Series history. The title chase proved to be one of the closest

Veteran Rick Crawford, shown here pitting his No. 14 Circle Bar Ford at Dover, posted his best NASCAR Craftsman Truck Series season in 2002, finishing second in the final championship standings. The likable Alabama driver went winless on the season, but managed 17 top-10 finishes to earn the runner-up spot in the title chase. *Nigel Kinrade*

Mike Bliss and Dave Fuge had reason to smile after winning the 2002 NASCAR Craftsman Truck Series championship. Bliss, out of work in 2001, and Fuge, suspended by NASCAR until the fifth race of the 2002 season, teamed to beat the odds and win the first of two-consecutive series championships for Express Motorsports. *High Sierra*

After making his first series start behind the wheel of the No. 63 Mittler Brothers Ford at Memphis Motorsports Park in 2002, Carl Edwards became the full-time driver of the No. 99 Roush Racing entry in 2003. Edwards won three times that season—at Kentucky Speedway, Indianapolis Raceway Park, and Nashville Superspeedway. His efforts earned him Raybestos Rookie of the Year honors. *Nigel Kinrade*

battles and most unusual championship finishes in series history. The championship came down to a final green, white, checkered-flag restart at Homestead where Musgrave seemingly beat both Kvapil and Setzer to the checkered flag.

After a protracted debate, NASCAR penalized Musgrave for passing to the left prior to the start/finish line on the restart and placed him 13th in the final running order—the last truck on the lead lap. That put Kvapil sixth and Setzer seventh in the race and gave Kvapil the championship by a mere nine points over Setzer and 18 over Musgrave, who finished third in the final standings.

"On the cool-down lap, my crew radioed me that Ted had jumped the restart and had gotten black-flagged," Kvapil said. "No one said what the penalty might be. Eventually, I was told NASCAR wanted me to pull down on the racetrack and prepare for the championship ceremony. It still was pretty unclear that we had been declared the championship team, and I

didn't want to stop at the start/finish line and have this thing pulled out from under me.

"I actually made one or two extra laps before NASCAR had me stop," he added. "NASCAR just wanted to look at the tapes and make the right call. It was then that I finally knew in my mind that I had won the championship, but it took 10 to 15 minutes to do it. It was pretty tense for a while, but when they told me I was the champion and I could get out of the truck, it felt like the weight of the world had been lifted off of my shoulders."

Kvapil, like Bliss the season before him, had beaten the odds and won a NASCAR Craftsman Truck Series championship. In 2004, an even longer bet—seeing a foreign make of vehicle in a NASCAR Victory Lane—would pay off big as Toyota made it a four-horse race for the NASCAR Craftsman Truck Series title.

Bill Lester's Dodge takes on left-side tires midway through the 2003 Craftsman 200 at Darlington. The race was the third of four series events held at the track between 2001 and 2004—two of which were won by Bobby Hamilton. At left, Hamilton is shown celebrating in Victory Lane after capturing the 2003 race at the famed speedway. *Nigel Kinrade*

Rick Crawford won his first NASCAR Craftsman Truck Series race at Homestead-Miami Speedway in 1998 and then waited 120 events before scoring his second victory in the 2003 Daytona 250. Here, an obviously overjoyed Crawford emerges from his ride in Victory Lane at Daytona. *High Sierra*

Rich Bickle (No. 9) leads Matt Crafton (No. 88), Darrell Waltrip (No. 17), Morgan Shepherd (No. 21), and Jon Wood (No. 50) into the first turn in the 2003 Advance Auto Parts 250 at Martinsville Speedway. Bickle, a series winner at Martinsville in 1997, finished eighth in the event. *Nigel Kinrade*

Jason Leffler's tenure behind the wheel of the No. 2 Team ASE Dodge lasted 38 races before he left the team after the 2003 Bristol event. Here, Leffler and Ultra Motorsports crew chief Tim Kohuth try to figure out what they need to do to make their truck faster. *Nigel Kinrade*

Tina Gordon competed in 13 NASCAR Craftsman Truck Series events in 2003, posting 13th-place finishes at Charlotte and Nashville as her season-best efforts. Female drivers Kelly Sutton, Shawna Robinson, and Teri MacDonald also competed in at least one series event during the 2003 season. *Nigel Kinrade*

Kevin Harvick enjoyed winning the 2002 NASCAR Craftsman Truck Series event at Phoenix International Raceway so much that he returned to do it again in 2003. Harvick, behind the wheel of the Looney Toons Chevy, led 80 of 150 laps in the 2003 event, taking the checkered flag in front of Ted Musgrave, Dennis Setzer, Carl Edwards, and Bobby Hamilton. *Nigel Kinrade*

Brendan Gaughan—the 2002 NASCAR Craftsman Truck Series Raybestos Rookie of the Year—held a 26-point lead in the championship standings heading into the final event of the 2003 series season at Homestead-Miami Speedway. Gaughan, shown here with Rick Crawford before the final race, was involved in an accident while running fifth and had to settle for fourth in the title chase. *Nigel Kinrade*

Travis Kvapil is doused with champagne as he hoists the 2003 NASCAR Craftsman Truck Series championship trophy in Victory Lane at Homestead-Miami Speedway. Kvapil won the title by just nine points (3,837 to 3,828) over runner-up Dennis Setzer. *High Sierra*

Bobby Hamilton served notice that he would be a challenger for the 2004 NASCAR Craftsman Truck Series championship early in the season when he won the second race of the year at Atlanta. Bobby Hamilton, shown here racing in the No. 4 Square D Dodge against Travis Kvapil at Martinsville, won four times while en route to the 2004 series title.
Nigel Kinrade

CHAPTER 8

You've Got It, Toyota

For decades, about the only time you ever heard about a foreign car maker being involved in NASCAR would be when a real die-hard racing fan recalled an obscure win by Al Keller in a Jaguar XK120 on the Linden Airport road course in New Jersey in June 1954.

That all changed in early 2003 when rumors that Toyota would enter the NASCAR ranks were confirmed by the Japanese automaker. It would put its Tundra model up against other manufacturers' pickups in the NASCAR Craftsman Truck Series in 2004.

Like Dodge did in 1996, Toyota saw the series as a way to ease into NASCAR. The NASCAR Craftsman Truck Series was the perfect proving ground—the races were short, competitive, and not under the glare of the intense media spotlight that accompanies the NASCAR NEXTEL Cup Series.

The plan worked perfectly for the automaker, as the Toyota Tundra is now a fixture in the NASCAR Craftsman Truck Series' Victory Lane. The research and development data gained from racing the truck has also spurred Toyota to make the jump to the NASCAR NEXTEL Cup Series in 2007 with its Camry model.

Back in 2004, however, nothing was a given for Toyota and its new NASCAR entry.

"We only had Ford, Chevy, and Dodge in the garage area in 1995, and they were competitive," said Mike Skinner, who was set to return to the division in 2004 after being signed to drive one of the new Toyota entries. "Toyota came on board and the bar was raised again. They elevated it. Toyota made the Big Three step up to the plate a little bit more."

The No. 24 Toyota Tundra driven by Travis Kvapil was just one of several fielded by the Japanese manufacturer in 2004. Kvapil showed the brand was capable of running well right out of the box with an impressive third-place finish in the season-opening event at Daytona International Speedway. *Nigel Kinrade*

Mike Skinner, the most dominant driver over the first two years of the NASCAR Craftsman Truck Series, rejoined the division in 2004 as part of the Toyota Racing Development (TRD) program. Skinner finished 11th in the final 2004 season standings, winning two pole positions and posting nine top-10 finishes. *Nigel Kinrade*

Veteran NASCAR NEXTEL Cup Series and truck series driver Ted Musgrave said all the teams quickly took notice of Toyota's entry—especially Dodge. "Our ears perked up and our eyes opened wide knowing here comes something we know we are going to

have to work hard to beat," he said. "Toyota had the support, development, and engineering behind it. When you think about Toyota racing and the winning history they had overseas and in open-wheel cars here, bringing all that knowledge to the [NASCAR Craftsman] Truck Series was pretty big."

Along with Skinner, Travis Kvapil, David Reutimann, Robert Huffman, Shelby Howard, and Bill Lester became drivers for the new-to-NASCAR manufacturer. And high-profile owners including three-time NASCAR NEXTEL Cup Series champion Darrell Waltrip and NASCAR NEXTEL Cup team owner Bill Davis also chose Toyota trucks for their new teams.

For Kvapil, landing one of the coveted Toyota rides was yet another strange turn in his career. Inexplicably, he had been released as the driver of the No. 16 IWX truck, despite winning the championship the year before.

"Initially, I was going to return to the IWX truck and we were going to try to run two trucks, with Jack Sprague in the second one," Kvapil said. "But Dave [Fuge] and Steve [Coulter] were having trouble finding sponsorship for the second truck and when it came right down to it, Jack was in and I was out. Two days after winning the championship at Miami, I was back at the same track where I had won the championship testing a new Toyota with a different group of guys. It was pretty strange."

Throughout the garage area, drivers and teams expressed concern about Toyota spending exorbitant amounts of money to dominate the division. When the trucks finally hit the track at Daytona for the 2004 preseason test, it was easy to see that big budget or not, the new kids on the block had their work cut out for them.

"We did the Daytona test with a brand new truck and we were around 25th on the time sheet," Kvapil said. "The speed just wasn't there and we were pretty discouraged. We took our truck back to

the shop and cut the body off of it. We basically started over because we needed to find some speed. We never questioned the engines. When we came back for the race and the money was on the line, the horsepower [Toyota] gave us was substantially better. It was like, 'Holy cow, this is what we needed all along under the hood.' We never thought they would have mule engines for testing. Toyota wasn't worried; it knew we had the horsepower needed when the time came."

When the green flag dropped at Daytona, a Ford led the 36-truck field into the first turn as Terry Cook surprised everyone by winning the pole in the Power Stroke Diesel–sponsored F-150 with a speed of 183.643 miles per hour.

Fellow Ford driver, and the previous season's Raybestos Rookie of the Year, Carl Edwards won the big race. Kvapil, Mike Wallace, Rick Crawford, and Cook completed the top five in another close event that saw Edwards win by a slim 0.141-second margin.

While Edwards was doing his now trademark back flip off the side of his truck in Victory Lane, Kvapil and the rest of the Toyota crowd were doing flips of their own back in the Daytona garage area following their second-place finish.

"We were knocking on the door right out of the box," Kvapil said. "We were never told to hold back by Toyota. Toyota had done the homework, doing all the R&D itself. Toyota

You couldn't wipe the grin off Carl Edwards' face after the Roush Racing driver captured the 2004 season-opening 250-mile NASCAR Craftsman Truck Series event at Daytona International Speedway. Edwards led 28 of 100 laps, taking the lead for good when he passed Frank Kimmel on the 80th lap. Edwards won more than $86,000 for his fourth career NASCAR Craftsman Truck Series victory. *High Sierra*

Speeding Up Truck Sales

The advent of the NASCAR Craftsman Truck Series in 1994 presented a ripe marketing opportunity for Detroit to cozy up to the buying public. Full-size pickup trucks had been evolving for years, offering a more car-like ride, better handling, and more comfort features. Trucks were no longer just workhorse hauling and towing vehicles—they were now personal vehicles to be pampered, polished, and customized. As such, they were among the hottest sellers in the automotive industry in the 1990s.

So just like in 1949—when NASCAR's first "strictly stock" car race was held and manufacturers learned that if they won on Sunday, they could sell their vehicles on Monday—truck manufacturers knew that if they could find on-track success in NASCAR's newest series it would translate to increased sales.

Ford and Chevrolet were the first truck makers to back the fledgling NASCAR Craftsman Truck Series, quickly tooling up for the inaugural 1995 season by providing well-funded, factory-supported efforts fielded by NASCAR NEXTEL Cup Series team owners like Richard Childress and Rick Hendrick. Meanwhile, top NASCAR NEXTEL Cup Series drivers Darrell Waltrip, Dale Earnhardt, Geoffrey Bodine, and Ernie Irvan also entered trucks with factory backing on a regular basis in 1995.

Dodge, meanwhile, had no factory involvement in 1995, but did supply trucks to several teams like the K-Automotive entry driven by longtime ARCA Series veteran and Mopar campaigner Bob Keselowski.

Campaigning a C/K 1500 model, the Chevy teams had the most success in the inaugural 1995 NASCAR Craftsman Truck Series season, winning the first eight races before Joe Ruttman drove a Ford F-150 to its initial series win at Bristol. In all, the Fords of Ruttman, Butch Miller, and Mike Bliss produced four wins for the Blue Oval gang in 1995, but it was Chevy who dominated the new division with 16 victories—eight by Mike Skinner alone—earning the first manufacturer's championship.

Meanwhile, the Dodge 1500 entries of "privateers" like Keselowski struggled without manufacturer's assistance, scoring no victories in 1995. The shutout wasn't totally unexpected, as unlike its Chevy and Ford counterparts, Dodge hadn't been an active supporter of NASCAR racing since the late 1970s. If Dodge was to be a player in the new division, the truck maker would have to step up its involvement.

Wide acceptance of the new division—along with the on-track success of Ford and Chevy in 1995—all but forced Dodge's hand to enter the series as a supporting manufacturer for the 1996 season. The move not only allowed Dodge and its Ram line of pickups to compete both on the track and on the showroom floor for bragging rights, but it also gave the Chrysler Corporation the platform it needed to develop NASCAR technology, setting the stage for the company to make the jump to the NASCAR NEXTEL Cup Series ranks in 2001.

Dodge entered the 1996 NASCAR Craftsman Truck Series season with a strong lineup that included the No. 43

Dodge Ram fielded by legendary Mopar racer Richard Petty. Petty and Dodge had been synonymous during the 1960s and 1970s, giving the new Dodge truck racing effort instant recognition and credibility with the truck-buying public.

Petty's truck, driven by Rich Bickle, had a solid season, earning Dodge its first NASCAR pole in two decades at Portland in May. Bickle eventually finished 11th in the season standings on the strength of five top-5 finishes.

In addition to Bickle, the Dodge factory–supported camp in 1996 included Bob Keselowski, Walker Evans, Jimmy Hensley, Lance Norick, and Michael Dokken. While the Dodge entries went winless in 1996, each driver finished in the top 20 in points at season's end. Hensley's eighth-place effort was the best of the group.

All three makes gained some common competitive ground as NASCAR instituted body template tech procedures as the truck series graduated to the superspeedways in the later 1990s. Despite the more common rules and shapes of the trucks, Chevy was able to continue its dominance, winning four-straight manufacturer's championships from 1995 to 1998. During that span, Chevy won a staggering 65 of the 97 races contested.

Ford finally showed its winning form in 1999, as young gun Greg Biffle scored nine of the brand's 12 victories while en route to Ford's first truck series manufacturer's championship.

Dodge, meanwhile, struggled to win races in its first five full seasons in the NASCAR Craftsman Truck Series, capturing just 14 victories in 146 division events before it captured its first manufacturer's championship in 2001.

Heading into the 2006 season, Chevy was still the dominant brand on the racetrack, scoring 120 total truck series wins—50 more than Ford and 56 greater than Dodge. Toyota's 13 wins during the 2004 and 2005 seasons have made the brand a player in the manufacturer's championship. It finished just one victory behind Chevy in 2005.

Chevy owned six NASCAR Craftsman Truck Series Manufacturer's Championships heading into 2006,

Chrysler Corporation and its Dodge truck brand returned to NASCAR racing as a manufacturer supporting the NASCAR Craftsman Truck Series in 1996. Easily its most visible team was the Richard Petty–owned entry driven by Rich Bickle, pictured here before the season-opening event at Homestead-Miami Speedway. *High Sierra*

It was a big day for Dodge as Rich Bickle won the pole for the third race of the year at Portland. Here, team owner Richard Petty and Bickle are honored for being the fastest qualifiers by Owen Kearns, series communications manager. Also shown are the Portland Speedway trophy queen and Dodge Racing representative Bob Wildberger. *High Sierra*

while Dodge had captured three and Ford had two titles. Given the near miss by Toyota in the 2005 manufacturer's chase and the brand's early domination of 2006 campaign, it won't be long before Toyota adds its name to the truck maker championship honor roll.

Toyota's success in the NASCAR Craftsman Truck Series has led to rumors that Nissan is considering bringing its full-size Titan pickup to the division in the near future. Only time will tell how many brands will populate the division, which is seen more and more as an entry point to greater NASCAR participation by vehicle manufacturers.

NASCAR Craftsman Truck Series rookie driver David Reutimann was the first to win a pole position for Toyota when he took the top spot at Atlanta with a lap of 179.452 miles per hour. Reutimann—the eventual Raybestos Rookie of the Year in 2004—finished third in the Atlanta event. *Nigel Kinrade*

The second 2004 race at Martinsville proved to be an off day for Hark Parker Jr. (No. 21), Kelly Sutton (No. 02), and David Reutimann (No. 17) as the trio got together on the front stretch during the early stages of the Kroger 200. *Nigel Kinrade*

pretty much gave us a turn-key truck. It didn't leave you a lot of room to mess it up."

"It was a big goal of each Toyota truck team to be the one to win the first race for Toyota," he added. "I really believed someone was going to do it early because of the equipment Toyota was giving us, especially after I ran second at Daytona and Mike [Skinner] was second at Atlanta a couple of weeks later."

At first, Skinner had doubted how fast the Japanese manufacturer could make its mark in the NASCAR ranks, but after Daytona, where

he had a chance to win and Kvapil finished second, he started to reconsider.

"We went to Atlanta and I finished second. It was like 'Man, we ain't ran but two races and this is pretty big,' " he said. "My whole thought process went from being negative to [believing] this was going to work."

While Toyota was working out the kinks in its new racing venture, Bobby Hamilton was quietly putting together a solid season that would ultimately earn him the 2004 NASCAR Craftsman Truck Series championship.

By the middle of the 2004 NASCAR Craftsman Truck Series season, team owner Jack Roush already had plans to move Carl Edwards to the NASCAR NEXTEL Cup Series. Edwards, who finished fourth in the final 2004 standings, first made that jump in August 2004, when he ran his first NASCAR NEXTEL Cup Series race at Michigan and finished 10th. *Nigel Kinrade*

The longtime NASCAR NEXTEL Cup Series regular had joined the truck series full time in 2003 and only had to coast to a 16th-place finish in the final 2004 event at Homestead-Miami to secure the title. The accomplishment was particularly sweet for Hamilton, who owned the team as well as drove for it. It was the first time since 1992 (when the late Alan Kulwicki captured the NASCAR NEXTEL Cup title) that an owner-driver had captured a major NASCAR championship.

Kvapil and the No. 24 Tundra proved to be the top Toyota entry in the manufacturer's first year of NASCAR Craftsman Truck Series compe-

tition, finishing eighth in the final season standings. More importantly, the team became the first to take a foreign entry to Victory Lane when Kvapil captured the Line-X 200 at Michigan International Speedway on July 31—more than 50 years after Al Keller had won in his Jaguar.

"We all had chances to win the first race for Toyota, but I got to be the one to do it at Michigan," Kvapil said. "It was a wild weekend because we had an engine change before the race, and I had to start the race at the back of the pack. I had to race Ted Musgrave and Mike Skinner for the win, but we had such a good truck and won in the final laps. It was so cool to pull into

Victory Lane, to see both mine and Mike Skinner's team there, all the Toyota folks, too. . . . You couldn't have asked for a better day."

The NASCAR Craftsman Truck Series also had a good year. The division, somewhat lost in the overwhelming promotional weight of the stick-and-ball sports on ESPN, was moved to SPEED TV in the 2004 season. The new network, while not reaching the number of households that ESPN did, made truck racing its No. 1 programming entity, heavily promoting the series throughout its regular telecast schedule.

Those promotional efforts spilled over onto the new network association the NASCAR NEXTEL Cup Series and NASCAR

There was plenty of competition among the Toyota teams to be the first to score a NASCAR Craftsman Truck Series win for the manufacturer. Travis Kvapil proved to be the first to do it as he wheeled the No. 24 Line-X Bed Liners–sponsored Tundra to win at Michigan on July 31, 2004. Kvapil is shown here celebrating the victory as he exits his truck and with his team in Victory Lane. *High Sierra* caption to come

For the second-straight season, Dennis Setzer finished second in the NASCAR Craftsman Truck Series championship standings, finishing 46 points—the same number as his truck—behind title winner Bobby Hamilton. Setzer won two times in 2004 and notched 16 top-10 finishes in 25 series events. *Nigel Kinrade*

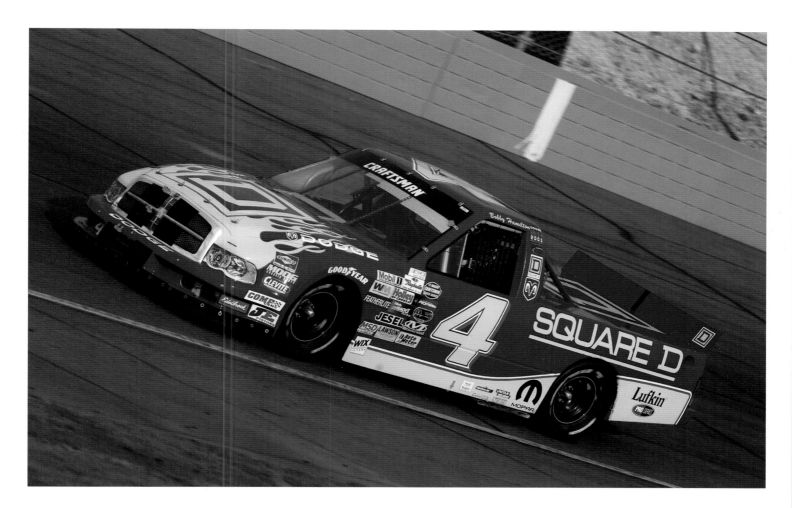

Busch Series employed with FOX and NBC in 2004. Suddenly, it was now common to see a commercial or promotional reference touting the next NASCAR Craftsman Truck Series race during NASCAR NEXTEL Cup Series and NASCAR Busch Series telecasts. In some instances, the references to the truck events were spilling over to National Football League games and prime-time programming on FOX.

Clearly, truck racing was now considered on par with the NASCAR NEXTEL Cup Series and NASCAR Busch Series in the eyes of the public. The malaise of earlier in the decade was long forgotten and the NASCAR Craftsman Truck Series was headed for bigger and better things as it prepared to race into the next 10 years of its existence.

After spending most of his career in the NASCAR NEXTEL Cup Series, Bobby Hamilton captured the 2004 NASCAR Craftsman Truck Series championship. Hamilton's Dodge finished in the top five in 12 of the 25 season races and collected nearly $1 million in prize money. Hamilton also got to take home some nice hardware at the banquet in Miami. *Nigel Kinrade/High Sierra*

The NASCAR Craftsman Truck Series made its debut at Lowe's Motor Speedway in 2003 and the track has been a part of the series schedule ever since. Here, Mike Skinner and Rick Crawford pound their trucks into the corner at more than 180 miles per hour in the 2005 race at the Charlotte area track. *Nigel Kinrade*

CHAPTER 9

10 Years Tough

Longtime NASCAR NEXTEL Cup Series and NASCAR Busch Series veterans Robert Pressley, Todd Bodine, Steve Park, Jimmy Spencer, Johnny Benson Jr., and Ricky Craven gave the NASCAR Craftsman Truck Series a boost as they joined the division full time in 2005. While some callously called the NASCAR Craftsman Truck Series "Cup Lite" or "The Seniors Tour," the fact of the matter was the division had reached an unequalled degree of competition.

"It's amazing how competitive it is now," said Mike Bliss, who also rejoined the truck series late in the 2005 season. "You're out there running good, but you are 15th and not going anywhere."

While there were plenty of new, high-profile faces in the division, it was just like old times when Ron Hornaday Jr., Jack Sprague, and Mike Skinner sat near the back of Skinner's hauler and swapped racing stories during testing for the 2005 season-opening Daytona 250.

Hornaday had returned full time to the truck series behind the wheel of Kevin Harvick's No. 6 Chevy, after Sprague and Skinner had returned a season earlier. The NASCAR Craftsman Truck Series had come

full circle now that its three greatest champions were back in the fold.

"When I had the opportunity to go back to the truck series, I said 'hell yeah,'" Skinner said. "You don't make near the money, but it's a lot better time. Now there are twenty drivers [who] can win each race. When I was here the first time, you had five drivers for sure—ten on a good day—[who] were really a threat to win. You could have a spin or a flat tire, go to the back, and cut your way back through to the top 10. Now it's

Ricky Craven was among the newcomers to the NASCAR Craftsman Truck Series in 2005. After a successful career in the NASCAR NEXTEL Cup Series and NASCAR Busch Series ranks, he won one event that season—the Kroger 200 at Martinsville—and finished 14th in the final truck series season standings. *Nigel Kinrade*

Jack Sprague injured his ankle in a household accident a month before the 2005 Atlanta race. Despite being on crutches outside of the No. 16 IWX Chevy, Sprague managed to finish eighth in the World Financial Group 200. *Nigel Kinrade*

not like that anymore. You get to 20th place, you hit a wall. It's twice as hard as it used to be."

Flying under the promotional banner of "The NASCAR Craftsman Truck Series— 1995–2005—10 Years Tough," the division opened the season with more fanfare and exposure than at any other time in its history. Again Daytona was the site of the first race, but the inaugural race also had a twist. It was run at night for the first time on the famed 2.5-mile oval.

Not only were ex-NASCAR NEXTEL Cup Series drivers flocking to the series in 2005, but so were a host of former team members. Here, longtime NASCAR NEXTEL Cup Series crew chief Mike Beam holds an impromptu meeting with his Roush Racing team on pit road at Martinsville. *John Close*

Team owners DeLana and Kevin Harvick celebrate with Ron and Lindy Hornaday after Hornaday won the 2005 World Financial Group 200 event at Atlanta Motor Speedway. The win was the 27th of Hornaday's storied NASCAR Craftsman Truck Series career. *Nigel Kinrade*

Bobby Hamilton was the first to strike, winning the Daytona 250 when it was deemed he made the late-pass of Jimmy Spencer before the final caution flag of the race flew, just after he and Spencer took the white flag.

Steve Park was the next ex–NASCAR NEXTEL Cup Series regular to break through, scoring a popular win at California the following week before Hornaday upped his NASCAR Craftsman Truck Series win record to 27 with his only victory of the season at Atlanta.

The NASCAR NEXTEL Cup Series connection to Victory Lane in truck events continued in

the fourth race of the season at Martinsville, but this time it was 2005 NASCAR NEXTEL Cup regular Bobby Labonte dropping down to score his first truck series win. Ted Musgrave's first victory of the season at Gateway and Hamilton's second at Mansfield competed the run of drivers with a link to the NASCAR NEXTEL Cup Series winning in truck racing before 18-year-old Kyle Busch won back-to-back events at Charlotte and Dover behind the wheel of Billy Ballew's No. 15 Chevy.

Mike Skinner showed he still knew the way to Victory Lane when he captured two events in

One of the most popular wins of the 2005 season came at California Speedway when Steve Park was victorious in the American Racing Wheels 200. Park, who had battled back from several devastating racing injuries, won the event behind the wheel of the No. 62 Jasper Engines and Transmissions Dodge fielded by Orleans Racing. *High Sierra*

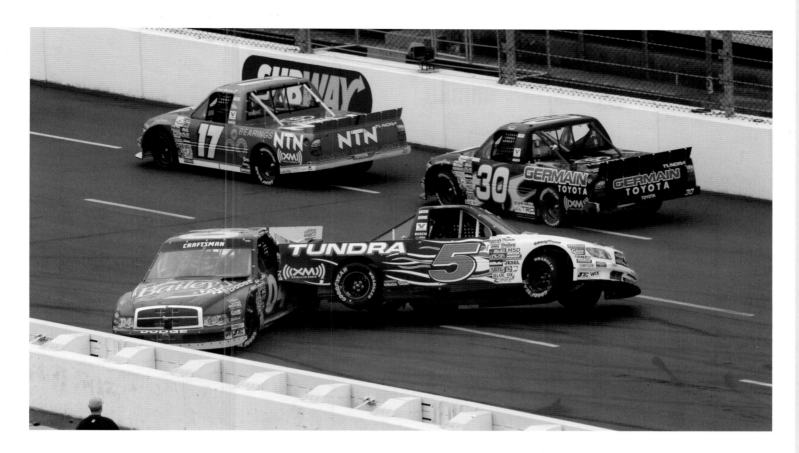

Mike Skinner, in the No. 5 Toyota Tundra, gets airborne as the truck tangles with the No. 04 Dodge driven by Bobby Hamilton during the 2005 Kroger 250 at Martinsville Speedway. Skinner recovered to finish ninth in the event, which Bobby Labonte won. *Nigel Kinrade*

Bill Lester joined the NASCAR Craftsman Truck Series on a full-time basis in 2002 and has been a staple of the division ever since. Lester also made his NASCAR NEXTEL Cup Series debut in 2006, wheeling a Bill Davis–owned Dodge in the Golden Corral 500 at Atlanta Motor Speedway. *Nigel Kinrade*

a row, at Bristol (his first in the division since winning at Mesa Marin in October 1996) and at Richmond.

The final three races of the season belonged to Todd Bodine as he rolled to wins at Texas, Phoenix, and Homestead, giving Toyota nine wins on the year, just one fewer than Chevy.

Meanwhile, longtime NASCAR Craftsman Truck Series standout Dennis Setzer was quietly putting together another solid season. The runner-up to Travis Kvapil and Hamilton in the final championship standings the previous two years, Setzer won at Michigan in June and then stomped the field in the following race at Milwaukee, where he lapped all but three trucks in the impressive victory. Another win two

The No. 1 Ultra Motorsports entry driven by Ted Musgrave is shown here getting the once over in the NASCAR Craftsman Truck Series tech line at Charlotte. Musgrave passed muster both in the inspection process and on the track. He scored 16 top-10 finishes while en route to the 2005 series championship. *John Close*

races later at Kentucky and a triumph at Indianapolis Raceway Park—his fourth win in his last six races—gave Setzer a seemingly insurmountable 227-point lead over Musgrave in the season standings with just 10 races left in the 25-race schedule.

Musgrave wasn't conceding anything, however, putting on a charge over the final 10 races while Setzer inexplicably slumped. When the final season points were tallied, Musgrave clinched the title by a 55-point margin over Setzer (3,535 to 3,480). The championship gave Musgrave the distinction of being the oldest NASCAR national touring series champion ever. He was 49 years and 11 months old.

In a statistical anomaly, the championship was the first for a vehicle carrying the No. 1 in any of NASCAR's top-three racing divisions.

Musgrave's championship also completed the circle for team owner Jim Smith. After fielding entries in 272 NASCAR Craftsman Truck Series events beginning in 1994 and ending with the 2005 Homestead event, the series pioneer finally had a championship.

"I don't think this is any surprise to anybody that this is one of my highest accomplishments in

Jimmy Spencer looks a bit perplexed as he tries to figure out the right setup for the No. 2 Team ASE Dodge at Charlotte. Spencer, one of several former NASCAR NEXTEL Cup Series drivers to compete in the truck series in 2005, ran in the top five in points for most of the season. But a 25th-place finishing average over the final six races of the year saddled him with a 12th-place standing in the championship chase. *John Close*

Kyle Busch first entered the NASCAR Craftsman Truck Series in 2001 as a 16-year-old kid, but changes in the driver age rule forced the Las Vegas, Nevada, driver to sit out until the 2004 season. Busch competed in 11 series races in 2005. He won three of them, including the Quaker Steak and Lube 200 at Lowe's Motor Speedway. Busch, shown here in Victory Lane after that event, became the series' youngest winner a few days after his 20th birthday. Busch scored a repeat win at Charlotte in 2006. *Nigel Kinrade*

Bowling Green, Kentucky, native Deborah Renshaw was a full-time NASCAR Craftsman Truck Series competitor in 2005, racing in all but one of the 25 division events. Her best finish of the year came at Dover where she drove the No. 8 Bobby Hamilton Racing Dodge to a 12th-place finish. *Nigel Kinrade*

Todd Kluever proved to be one of the surprises of the 2005 NASCAR Craftsman Truck Series season. The Sun Prairie, Wisconsin, driver notched a trio of second-place finishes—at Kansas, O'Reilly Raceway Park, and Martinsville—and finished 11th in the final championship standings. That performance earned Kleuver the division's Raybestos Rookie of the Year award. *Nigel Kinrade*

motorsports," Smith said after the Miami championship clincher. "We've won a lot of races, led a lot of laps, the most poles. We've done it all, and this has eluded us for years. It's something I'm going to cherish. I wanted it desperately. I think whatever you're racing you always want to be No. 1 in your sport. We achieved that today."

Musgrave's title came against the most competitive field of trucks and drivers in the history of the NASCAR Craftsman Truck Series. The "10 Years Tough" motto of the division had lived up to its name as the influx of former NASCAR NEXTEL Cup Series stars and former truck series champions were now battling for a spot in Victory Lane at every race. The groundwork for a second decade of competition–bigger and better than ever–was in place and stuck on full throttle.

Ted Musgrave, driver of the No. 1 Mopar Performance Parts Dodge, gets some extra attention in the garage area at Richmond. Musgrave, who won his first NASCAR NEXTEL Cup Series pole at Richmond in 1994, started third and finished fourth in the 2005 Richmond NASCAR Craftsman Truck Series event. *John Close*

Todd Bodine dominated the late stages of the 2005 NASCAR Craftsman Truck Series season by winning four of the final six races, including the last three. Bodine also got a quick start in the 2006 season, taking wins in the first three of the nine races. *Nigel Kinrade*

Ted Musgrave became the oldest champion in the history of NASCAR when the Franklin, Wisconsin, driver captured the 2005 NASCAR Craftsman Truck Series title. Musgrave was just a little over one month shy of his 50th birthday when he celebrated his championship with series pioneer and longtime team owner Jim Smith. *High Sierra*

One of the wildest accidents in the NASCAR Craftsman Truck Series in recent years happened in the fourth-to-last race of the 2005 season at Atlanta. Steve Park (No. 67) lost control of the Dodge he was driving as the field headed into Turn One on the second lap of the race. The trucks driven by Mike Bliss (No. 16) and Eric Norris (No. 07) got caught up in the melee. The high-speed impact with the wall sent all three trucks spinning through the turn where the IWX Chevy driven by Bliss broke into flames. While Norris skidded down the track and out of harm's way, the speed of the incident carried the trucks of Park and Bliss all the way to the exit of Turn Two before both drivers were able to climb out uninjured. *High Sierra*

Whether it's on the short tracks or the superspeedways, many veteran racing observers
agree that the close quarters racing in the series is the best NASCAR has to offer.
High Sierra

CHAPTER 10

Truckin' in the Future

The dawn of the NASCAR Craftsman Truck Series' second decade in 2006 was light years away from the 1995 inaugural campaign.

In the beginning, nobody knew if the division would have enough trucks or drivers to compete, much less if anyone would show up to watch. Those questions now have been long forgotten, as more than 500 drivers have competed in the series' first 10 years. Along the way, the truck series has grown into the third-largest racing series in the United States, drawing millions of spectators to the track while positioning itself as the most-viewed programming on SPEED TV.

"I think the [NASCAR Craftsman] Truck Series has developed solidly into a good—no, a great national series," NASCAR CEO Brian France said, reflecting on its first decade in existence. "It has a mix of young and old drivers. Our most diehard fans will probably tell you that it's probably the best racing among the three national divisions. It has a solid television draw on SPEED; it's their No. 1 show. You can always do better, but it's a very solid division."

So solid that the NASCAR Craftsman Truck Series added Talladega Superspeedway to the scheduling mix in 2006. The 2.66-mile oval, the largest on the NASCAR tour, joined Daytona, California, Atlanta, Gateway, Charlotte, Dover, Texas, Michigan, Milwaukee, Kansas, Kentucky, Nashville, New Hampshire, Las Vegas, Phoenix, and Miami-Homestead as tracks more than a mile in length.

Meanwhile, Martinsville, Bristol, Memphis, Mansfield, and O'Reilly Raceway Park were the only short tracks left in the series that opened with 14 of them on the schedule in 1995.

Larger tracks, like Michigan International Speedway pictured here, will continue to rule the NASCAR Craftsman Truck Series schedule as the division draws more fans and a wider acceptance base.
High Sierra

O'Reilly Raceway Park at Indianapolis continues to be one of the few short tracks that remains on the NASCAR Craftsman Truck Series tour.
High Sierra

The influx of NASCAR NEXTEL Cup Series drivers like Mark Martin, shown here buckling up before winning the 2006 series race at Daytona, can only help the NASCAR Craftsman Truck Series gain a greater fan base and more attention in the media.
John Close

"I'm a little disappointed that the series has left the short tracks and has gone where it's at," said Gary Collins, who constructed the original truck and finished second in the division's first exhibition race at Bakersfield. "I can understand it, but I really liked it on the half-mile and mile tracks.

"I still keep up with the series quite a bit. I look back and feel like we did something. We built something from the ground up here in Bakersfield that has now become the third-largest racing series in the country," he added. "Nobody would have ever guessed that when we first started."

"Personally, I'd like to see us stay on the short tracks and at places like Richmond, but I understand why NASCAR is taking us to places like Talladega," Ron Hornaday Jr. added. "If

you look at what NASCAR has done with this series over the past 10 to 11 years, you'd have to say they know what they are doing. You have to remember that when the NASCAR Craftsman Truck Series started, we stopped halfway [through the race], got out of the truck, went to the bathroom, got back in, and finished the race. I think you can say we've come a long way since then."

While the on-track action has always been a big draw of the series, the addition of NASCAR NEXTEL Cup Series drivers such as Ted Musgrave, Bobby Hamilton, Jimmy

Spencer, Ricky Craven, Robert Pressley, Todd Bodine, and Johnny Benson Jr. also boosted the credibility and media profile of the division with the fans.

"With the influx of ex-NASCAR NEXTEL Cup drivers into the series, their fans have come along for the ride and the NASCAR Craftsman Truck Series is getting more exposure than ever," said longtime division competitor Terry Cook. "We're going to have another huge leap in popularity when guys like Mark Martin start coming here full time in 2007. As long as more NASCAR NEXTEL Cup

The days of towing a small trailer and bringing a few crewmembers to the racetrack have long disappeared from the NASCAR Craftsman Truck Series. In recent years, the greatest increase in the cost of competing in the division hasn't been the hardware, but the rising cost of crew salaries. *John Close*

The NASCAR Craftsman Truck Series has evolved into a big-time motorsports division with all the pomp and circumstance formerly reserved for the bigger NASCAR NEXTEL Cup Series and NASCAR Busch Series. Here, teams line up for prerace ceremonies prior to an event at Gateway International Raceway near St. Louis, Missouri. *High Sierra*

Series drivers 'retire' to the truck series, you're going to see a lot of great racing and a lot more growth to the division. I don't think anyone ever expected the truck series would be this popular to begin with. Now it's hard to imagine NASCAR racing without it."

The numbers back Cook's statements. Even though the crowd at the first exhibition race at Mesa Marin in 1995 featured a packed house, that throng of 5,000 or so pales in comparison to the more than 100,000 fans who watched Martin win the first race of the 2006 campaign at Daytona. According to Owen Kearns, the

only manager of communications for the NASCAR Craftsman Truck Series since its inception, getting to that level of popularity is a result of the division's ability to navigate through uncharted waters.

"A lot of trial and error that NASCAR never did before was done in the NASCAR Craftsman Truck Series," Kearns said. "Things like green-, white-, checkered-flag finishes, inverted starts, and half-time breaks couldn't be experimented with in the NASCAR NEXTEL Cup Series. We could do that kind of stuff in the truck series because we didn't have any

Matt Smela, from International Engine Company's Power Stroke Diesel division, is shown here conducting a pit tour for a group of corporate associates. As long as corporate America finds promotional value in motorsports and pickup trucks, the NASCAR Craftsman Truck Series is going to be a major player in the national motorsports scene. *John Close*

Drivers like Ted Musgrave have revitalized their careers after moving to the NASCAR Craftsman Truck Series. Musgrave, shown here in the No. 9 Germain Racing Toyota, is one of the top stars in the division and captured the 2005 championship. *John Close*

It took only a decade for the NASCAR Craftsman Truck Series to grow from humble beginnings as a short-track novelty to a featured attraction at the nation's premier raceways. Here's a shot of the trucks under clear Florida skies in the garage area at the 2006 Daytona race. *John Close*

Ted Musgrave (No. 9) leads Mike Skinner (No. 5), Mark Martin (No. 6), Ron Hornaday Jr. (No. 33), Rick Crawford (No. 14), and Bill Lester (No. 22) through the tri-oval at Daytona International Speedway early in the 2006 Daytona 250 NASCAR Craftsman Truck Series race. Note the packed front-stretch grandstand as the race drew more than 100,000 spectators and millions more watched the action on television. *Nigel Kinrade*

history. Some of it worked, some of it we did for a couple of races and then dropped it because it didn't work. People didn't mind us doing that kind of stuff because we weren't messing with traditions that might have dated back to 1956."

"I never thought the truck series was going to be what it is today," added Jim Smith, one of the four pioneers to envision the division. "It was going to be an opportunity for a lot of people without a lot of money to go racing. It grew so fast right from the start. You take a look at the talent that was in the lineup at the very

first race at Phoenix and you knew that it was going to be something special."

However, for all its progress, the NASCAR Craftsman Truck Series has lost some of what initially made it unique. The move to superspeedways, the costs associated with that transition, and a decade of escalated competition issues has changed the division forever.

Among those affected by the growing cost of competition is Smith, who shut down his Ultra Motorsports team just barely a month after finally winning a championship in 2005.

After making just three career NASCAR Craftsman Truck Series starts over the previous 10 seasons, NASCAR NEXTEL Cup Series star Mark Martin made an immediate impact in 2006 by winning the season-opening Daytona 250. Here, Martin gives the fans some old-school flavor by carrying the checkered flag around the track. *Nigel Kinrade*

"My biggest concern right now is the cost of running the series is way out of control," Smith said. "It takes five million dollars a year to run up front in the NASCAR Craftsman Truck Series now. That's the kind of dedication, time, and money you have to invest if you are going to be competitive in this thing."

"The biggest obstacle [to growth] will be the ability to overcome the cost of racing," series director Wayne Auton added. "I think you could say that for all of motorsports today. It's not a huge problem. We just have to make sure the owners can keep coming to the racetrack."

Cost containment aside, there are plenty of drivers who are willing to compete in truck racing. That's especially true of drivers like Mike Bliss and Jack Sprague who have made their mark in racing as stars of the division.

"We all want to race at the NASCAR NEXTEL Cup Series level and make tons of money, but sometimes it's just not worth the aggravation," Bliss said. "You're away from home a lot and money doesn't buy everything. When you walk in the NASCAR Craftsman Truck Series garage, your stomach doesn't get all knotted up. In the truck series, it's still fun. If

Veteran Mike Skinner (No. 5) and newcomer Brad Keselowski (No. 29) wage a side-by-side battle during the early stages of the 2006 Racetickets.com 200 at California Speedway. The series has long become fertile ground for experienced drivers like Skinner to earn a living while serving the needs of aspiring pilots like Keselowski, who are trying to break into the big leagues of NASCAR. *Nigel Kinrade*

you ask a lot of people, they'll tell you the trucks have the best racing. We've got it made here."

"Initially, I thought the trucks would just be a fad, a flash in the pan, never last," Sprague added. "I though it was just something where I could race and didn't have to spend my own money to do it. I never would have figured it would turn out to be what I have done most of my career."

Despite no longer being in the truck series, Smith is also proud of the fact the division has brought opportunities to so many racers and crewmembers throughout its existence.

"One of the things that's been most gratifying to me is to see how many people got jobs in NASCAR because of the truck series," he said. "You can go on and on about the drivers who have gone to the NASCAR NEXTEL Cup Series from the truck series—Mike Skinner, Greg Biffle, Ron Hornaday, Mike Bliss, Kevin Harvick, Kurt Busch, Carl Edwards, Scott Riggs. . . . And that's just the drivers. Just look around

Bobby Hamilton Jr. (No. 18) and Mark Martin (No. 6) lead the field to the green flag in the 2006 Kroger 250 at Martinsville Speedway. The younger Hamilton took over the seat of the No. 18 Dodge Ram when his father, 2004 NASCAR Craftsman Truck Series champion Bobby Hamilton, was diagnosed with cancer and had to sit out the remainder of the 2006 season. *Nigel Kinrade*

the truck garage. We created a tremendous amount of jobs and income for a lot of people. That's been a real fun side to all of this."

So what does the future hold for the NASCAR Craftsman Truck Series? Like those moments heading into the inaugural 1995 season, no one can tell for sure what will happen. But the influx of new, young talent and the desire of even more NASCAR NEXTEL Cup Series veterans like Mark Martin—who are willing to shift career gears and join the division—make for a bright horizon.

"For some reason, the trucks fit," Hornaday said. "All kinds of racers, guys like Mark Martin, want to come and race trucks now. It is hard racing, and here they treat you like you are somebody, like you are family. You can have a great time, have fun racing, and make a great living at it."

"I don't need a crystal ball to see where this is going," Musgrave added. "More people are tuning in to our races on television, more people are coming to the races, and we're getting more [NASCAR NEXTEL] Cup Series

Terry Cook pounds the No. 10 Power Stroke Diesel by the International Ford F-150 through the bottom groove during the 2006 Kroger 250 at Martinsville Speedway. Cook, a former winner at Martinsville, had a disappointing day this time around, finishing 19th. He visited Victory Lane later in the year at Kansas Speedway. *Nigel Kinrade*

drivers who can't wait to come over here and run this series. From when I came over here five years ago to now, you can see the hype that's coming on to this series. I'm glad I got in it when I did because it's becoming harder and harder to win these races. It's just going to grow each and every year."

Once a pipe dream of four individuals from California, the NASCAR Craftsman Truck Series has now become a vibrant part of the national motorsports landscape—a journey started in the remote desert and has now reached the largest of racing's stages.

In the end, current NASCAR CEO and President Brian France, who along with Dennis Huth and many others saw the potential in racing pickup trucks, was the NASCAR Craftsman Truck Series' biggest backer.

"Initially, it was a lot tougher than we thought, but you'd have to say it's all worked out for the best," France said. "The NASCAR Craftsman Truck Series filled a need, has been more successful than we ever dreamed, and is here to stay. It's been a real success story for everyone involved."

Championship Standings 1995–2005

1995

1	Mike Skinner	3,225
2	Joe Ruttman	3,098
3	Ron Hornaday Jr.	2,986
4	Butch Miller	2,812
5	Jack Sprague	2,740
6	Rick Carelli	2,683
7	Bill Sedgwick	2,681
8	Mike Bliss	2,626
9	Scott Lagasse	2,470
10	Toby Butler	2,358

1996

1	Ron Hornaday Jr.	3,831
2	Jack Sprague	3,778
3	Mike Skinner	3,771
4	Joe Ruttman	3,275
5	Mike Bliss	3,190
6	Dave Rezendes	3,179
7	Butch Miller	3,126
8	Jimmy Hensley	3,029
9	Bryan Reffner	2,961
10	Rick Carelli	2,953

1997

1	Jack Sprague	3,969
2	Rich Bickle	3,737
3	Joe Ruttman	3,736
4	Mike Bliss	3,611
5	Ron Hornaday Jr.	3,574
6	Jay Sauter	3,467
7	Rick Carelli	3,461
8	Jimmy Hensley	3,385
9	Chuck Bown	3,320
10	Kenny Irwin Jr.	3,220

1998

1	Ron Hornaday Jr.	4,072
2	Jack Sprague	4,069
3	Joe Ruttman	3,874
4	Jay Sauter	3,672
5	Tony Raines	3,596
6	Jimmy Hensley	3,570
7	Stacy Compton	3,542
8	Greg Biffle	3,276
9	Ron Barfield Jr.	3,227
10	Mike Bliss	3,216

1999

1	Jack Sprague	3,747
2	Greg Biffle	3,739
3	Dennis Setzer	3,639
4	Stacy Compton	3,623
5	Jay Sauter	3,543
6	Mike Wallace	3,494
7	Ron Hornaday, Jr.	3,488
8	Andy Houston	3,359
9	Mike Bliss	3,294
10	Jimmy Hensley	3,280

2000

1	Greg Biffle	3,826
2	Kurt Busch	3,596
3	Andy Houston	3,566
4	Mike Wallace	3,450
5	Jack Sprague	3,316
6	Joe Ruttman	3,278
7	Dennis Setzer	3,214
8	Randy Tolsma	3,157
9	Bryan Reffner	3,153
10	Steve Grissom	3,113

2001

1	Jack Sprague	3,670
2	Ted Musgrave	3,597
3	Joe Ruttman	3,570
4	Travis Kvapil	3,547
5	Scott Riggs	3,526
6	Ricky Hendrick	3,412
7	Terry Cook	3,327
8	Rick Crawford	3,320
9	Dennis Setzer	3,306
10	Coy Gibbs	2,875

2002

1	Mike Bliss	3,359
2	Rick Crawford	3,313
3	Ted Musgrave	3,308
4	Jason Leffler	3,156
5	David Starr	3,144
6	Dennis Setzer	3,132
7	Robert Pressley	3,097
8	Terry Cook	3,070
9	Travis Kvapil	3,039
10	Coy Gibbs	3,010

2003

1	Travis Kvapil	3,837
2	Dennis Setzer	3,828
3	Ted Musgrave	3,819
4	Brendan Gaughan	3,797
5	Jon Wood	3,659
6	Bobby Hamilton	3,627
7	Rick Crawford	3,578
8	Carl Edwards	3,416
9	Terry Cook	3,212
10	Chad Chaffin	3,143

2004

1	Bobby Hamilton	3,624
2	Dennis Setzer	3,578
3	Ted Musgrave	3,554
4	Carl Edwards	3,493
5	Matt Crafton	3,379
6	David Starr	3,298
7	Jack Sprague	3,167
8	Travis Kvapil	3,152
9	Steve Park	3,138
10	Chad Chaffin	3,122

2005

1	Ted Musgrave	3,538
2	Dennis Setzer	3,480
3	Todd Bodine	3,462
4	Ron Hornaday Jr.	3,369
5	Mike Skinner	3,273
6	Bobby Hamilton	3,164
7	David Starr	3,148
8	Jack Sprague	3,137
9	Matt Crafton	3,095
10	Johnny Benson Jr.	3,076

Index

About the Author: After years of covering late-model, short-track stock car races in his native Wisconsin as a daily newspaper reporter, John Close worked his first NASCAR race as a journalist at Bristol International Raceway in 1986. He joined the NASCAR community in 1994, serving as the public relations representative for Bobby Labonte's Maxwell House Coffee NASCAR NEXTEL Cup Series effort.

Close, whose articles have been published in top industry publications such as *Stock Car Racing* and *Circle Track* magazines, has specialized in covering the NASCAR Craftsman Truck Series since 1996 when he joined Richard Petty Motorsports as a public relations specialist.

Since then, he has participated in numerous NASCAR public relations and media initiatives for several top truck series racing teams, including Hendrick and Ultra Motorsports and front-running drivers Ted Musgrave, Scott Riggs, Rich Bickle, Terry Cook, Jason Leffler, Ricky Hendrick, and Jack Sprague. Close is also an active NASCAR raceday spotter, calling nearly 100 NASCAR NEXTEL Cup Series, NASCAR Busch Series, and NASCAR Craftsman Truck Series races over the past decade.

His first book, *Tony Stewart: From Indy Phenom to NASCAR Superstar,* was released by MBI Publishing Company in 2004.

He and his wife, Gail, and son, Sam, reside in Charlotte, North Carolina.